Sterilisation and Hygiene

Also published by Stanley Thornes (Publishers) Ltd:

W. E. Arnould-Taylor & A. Harris	*Principles and Practice of Electrology*
J. F. Rounce	*Science for the Beauty Therapist*
E. Almond	*Safety in the Salon*
A. Gallant	*Beauty Guide 4: Epilation Treatment*
J. Gardiner	*Cardiac Arrest – What do you do?*
J. Gardiner	*The ECG – What does it tell?*

Sterilisation and Hygiene

A Practical Guide for the Beauty,
Hairdressing and Health Care Professions

W. G. Peberdy F.R.Pharm.S.
Honorary technical adviser to the Institute of Electrolysis

Stanley Thornes (Publishers) Ltd

Text © W. G. Peberdy
Original line artwork © Stanley Thornes (Publishers) Ltd 1988

All rights reserved. No part of this publication may be reproduced, stored in a retrieval system or transmitted in any form or by any means, electronic, mechanical, photocopying, recording or otherwise, without the prior written consent of the copyright holders. Applications for such permission should be addressed to the publishers: Stanley Thornes (Publishers) Ltd, Old Station Drive, Leckhampton, CHELTENHAM, GL53 0DN, England.

First Published in 1988 by:
Stanley Thornes (Publishers) Ltd
Old Station Drive
Leckhampton
CHELTENHAM GL53 0DN
England

British Library Cataloguing in Publication Data

Peberdy, W.
   Sterilisation and hygiene: a practical
   guide for the beauty hairdressing and
   health care professions.
   1. Service industries. Hygiene
   I. Title
   613.6'2

ISBN 0-85950-900-1

Typeset by Tech-Set, Gateshead, Tyne & Wear
Printed and bound in Great Britain at The Bath Press, Avon

Contents

	Foreword	vii
	Acknowledgements	viii
	Introduction	ix
Chapter 1	**Bacteria**	**1**
	Structure	1
	Growth and reproduction	3
	Classification of bacteria	4
	Culture of bacteria	6
	Virulence	8
	Antigens and antibodies	8
	Common pathogenic bacteria	9
Chapter 2	**Viruses and other pathogenic organisms**	**16**
	Classification of viruses	16
	Structure and morphology	17
	Invasion of host cells	18
	Culture of viruses	20
	Identification of viruses in disease conditions	21
	Important pathogenic viruses	21
	Other pathogenic organisms	23
Chapter 3	**Infection and disease**	**29**
	Sources of infection	29
	Routes of infection	32
	The body's defences against infection	34
	Diseases which may be transmitted by beauty and health-care workers	36
Chapter 4	**Definitions**	**43**
	Sterilisation	43
	Disinfectant	44
	Antiseptic	44
	Bactericide	45
	Bacteriostat	45

	Virucide, Sporicide, Fungicide, Biocide	45
	Aseptic methods	46
	Antibiotic	46
Chapter 5	**Sterilisation**	**47**
	Tests for efficiency of sterilisation	48
	Cleaning of articles before sterilisation	49
	Sterilisation methods available	50
	Summary	65
Chapter 6	**Disinfectants and antiseptics**	**67**
	Disinfection and sterilisation	68
	Factors affecting chemical disinfectants and antiseptics	68
	Available substances	70
	Summary	82
Chapter 7	**Design of hygienic procedures for use in a practice**	**83**
	Basic considerations	83
	Disinfection and sterilisation of equipment	93
	Antiseptics for use on treated areas of clients	95
	Personal cleanliness and protection for operators	95
Chapter 8	**Self-examination questions**	**97**
	Answers to self-examination questions	110
Chapter 9	**Model by-laws**	**112**
Chapter 10	**Recommended supplementary reading**	**116**
Appendices	1 Microscopes	119
	2 Alkalinity and acidity	119
	3 Not an ideal clinic or salon!	120
	Index	**122**

Foreword

Since the use of needles, with the associated risk of cross-infection, is implicit in the practice of electrolysis, the Institute has always insisted on the highest standards of hygiene from its members. Nevertheless, with the advent of AIDS and the legislation following the 1982 Act it became apparent that a complete rethink of our procedures was urgently required.

I had known the author very well for more than 30 years, both as a pharmacist and as husband of one of our members and I knew that with his background, wide interests and adaptability he would be an ideal person to help us. I therefore invited him, in 1985, to talk about hygiene and sterilisation to members at the Institute's Annual General Meeting.

As a result of this talk he was invited to introduce the subject into the Institute's examination syllabus and then to become its examiner, adviser and a member of its Council. In this capacity he quickly became aware that, whilst it was easy to develop a suitable syllabus, no textbook existed to support this, so, characteristically, he set about writing one. The present volume is the outcome. He now devotes a considerable amount of time to the subject, having in addition become a consultant to a major company in the steriliser field.

I read the book in its early stages and found it readable, informative and progressive in presentation. I consider it essential reading for all professions in which a risk of cross-infection exists and it fills an obvious gap in the literature. It is a must, equally valuable for the established practitioner, the student and the teacher and is unique in its field.

W. L. Howard-Smith, M.C., D.R.E.,
Past Chairman, The Institute of Electrolysis,
Wakefield.
1988

Acknowledgements

Many people have helped me in various ways in preparing this book. In particular I should like to acknowledge the constructive criticism offered by my good friend Nevile Burwell, M.D., Ch.M., F.R.C.S. Our walks together in the Pennines have been enlivened by discussions on the lengths of sentences and paragraphs, the use of simple English, and the avoidance of the many pitfalls which await the embryo writer. My sincere thanks are due to Len Howard-Smith for writing the foreword and for focusing my thoughts on the necessity for this book, and also to my Publishers.

I am grateful to the following for supplying and giving permission to reproduce photographs:
Dr T. Brain/Science Photo Library, p. 10 (top); J. Durham/Science Photo Library, p. 10 (centre and bottom); Hospital Equipment and Laboratory Products Ltd, p. 56 (bottom); H. Morgan/Science Photo Library, p. 7; Prestige Medical, p. 61; Surgical Equipment Supplies Ltd, pp. 54, 60 (top and bottom); Taylor Reeson Laboratories, p. 56 (top).

Finally to my wife, Marion, who brought the subject of electrolysis into the family many years ago and is still a practising electrolysist. Without this introduction the book would never have been conceived and but for her tolerance during its long gestation, it would never have come to fruition.

W. G. Peberdy
Leeds, 1988.

Introduction

The object of this book is to provide concise information about sterilisation, disinfection and hygiene for those whose background is non-medical and whose scientific knowledge is limited. Many such persons are becoming involved in sterilising or disinfecting their equipment with little knowledge of what they are doing or why they are doing it.

Until quite recently, only hospital surgical units were seriously involved in this work although pharmacists and the pharmaceutical industry worked to high standards when necessary. Those in general medical and dental practice had only limited knowledge of what was required and their methods were often founded more on tradition than on sound scientific principles.

In the past two decades, wider knowledge of the routes by which hepatitis B is spread has been gained. The proven involvement of those in cosmetic skin-piercing work, such as tattooing and ear-piercing, and in acupuncture in such spread has been recognised and this has resulted in the registration and control of practitioners. Dentists are taking much greater precautions, both to protect their patients from cross-infection and to protect themselves and their staff. It seems likely that hairdressers will soon find themselves subject to legislation and their professional bodies are already recommending sterilisation of equipment.

With the advent of AIDS, there is a new surge of interest in safety precautions and this is now backed by a very real fear of cross-infection amongst the public. Clients are looking critically at those from whom they seek treatment and the latter are expected to discuss their precautions and the degree of risk involved.

Finally, enforcement of regulations is vested in the Environmental Health Departments of local authorities. The work of these officers is diverse and this is a new area for them.

This book is therefore aimed at two broad groups of persons.

The first group comprises beauty professionals and allied workers. This includes electrolysists, ear-piercers and tattooists, acupuncturists, chiropodists and manicurists, hairdressers and all beauty therapists who work on the skin.

The second group consists of health care workers in the broadest sense. It includes dental nurses, industrial first-aid staff, unqualified workers in clinics, etc., and all those who may be involved in hygienic work for other health professionals. Students in the food and catering industries will also find most of the material invaluable and relevant to their work.

Environmental Health Officers will find this book most useful as an introduction to their new responsibilities.

With the exception of Chapter 7, this book gives information which is general in nature and provides a simple introduction to the subject. Scientific terms are not excluded but they are explained in simple language which means that the interested reader can take up more advanced work with an understanding of the underlying principles. The background of bacteriology and virology is discussed and important diseases are explained.

The relevant terms are defined, followed by a full description of sterilisation methods. Disinfectants and antiseptics are considered and their properties described and compared. Throughout, the requirements of specific professions are emphasised where applicable.

The workers in the first group described above tend to be self-employed. Chapter 7 is aimed specifically at them and advises on the practical application of the principles learned in the running of their salons. Nevertheless it contains many lessons which will be of value to those in the second group who tend to work in an environment provided by an employer. For Environmental Health Officers it will provide a most valuable guide on the standards which they might reasonably expect in the work-place.

Chapter 8 has self-examination questions for readers to check what they have learned, whilst Chapter 10 recommends other books for more advanced study.

It is recommended that the book be read right through to give an overall picture of its contents. It can then be studied in more detail, chapter by chapter, perhaps using the self-examination questions to test knowledge gained. The detailed index will provide a useful reference when specific information is required subsequently.

CHAPTER 1

Bacteria

In taking up this book, most readers will be moving into a new sphere of knowledge. They may have seen documentary programmes on television about medical matters or read similar articles in the press. Such material will however have been fragmented. Sterilisation and hygiene are essentially about taking precautions. It would be easy to lay down a series of rules without explanation. Readers, however, will be working in a widely differing range of environments, even within the same profession. The products and equipment being used are changing and developing constantly. It is therefore essential that those who are going to carry out sterilisation and hygiene safely and successfully understand the implications of what they are doing.

As a background, some knowledge of bacteria, viruses and other infecting agents is valuable and this is provided in these first two chapters.

Bacteria are single-celled organisms, microscopic in size, which reproduce by dividing into two. This is called **binary fission**. They have properties common both to animals and plants. Higher animals and plants which have close similarities are grouped together. Bacteria vary quite widely from one another and are grouped together largely for convenience.

STRUCTURE

Bacterial cells are rigid – they keep their shape and do not sag or flow like some unicellular animals.

They consist of a **cell wall**, responsible for the shape and rigidity, and **protoplast**, the name given to the cell contents. The cell wall is very important. It offers protection against chemical and physical assault, and provides mechanical strength.

Most of the cells of animals contain a well-defined nucleus in which is concentrated the genetic material DNA (deoxyribonucleic acid). The DNA molecule is a double chain made up of vast numbers of simple chemical units. These units are grouped together into **genes**. The genes carry the information which identifies the particular animal and its species.

In bacterial cells there is no nucleus although DNA is present in the protoplast.

This DNA almost certainly governs the activity of the cell in the same way as in higher forms of life. Under its influence complex substances called **enzymes** are formed. These highly important substances control the metabolism of the cell.

Some bacteria have one or more long whip- or hair-like structures attached to their surface, which are known as **flagella**. These enable the organism to move when it is said to be **motile**. Some also have shorter, finer and more numerous threads known as **pili** or **fimbriae**.

In addition to the cell wall, certain bacteria have a thick gelatinous coat or outer layer called a **capsule**. This may be developed only in particular circumstances – for instance, some organisms form capsules in the tissues but not in cultures.

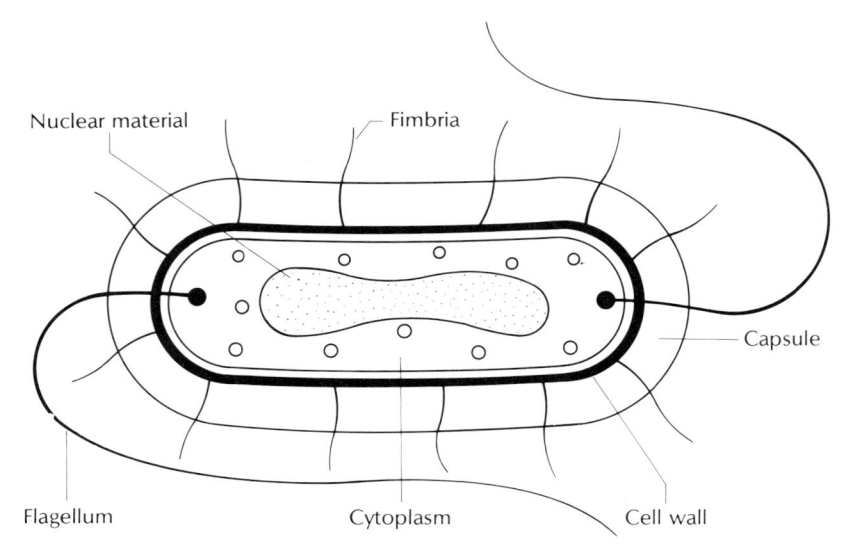

Basic features of a typical bacterial cell.

SPORE FORMATION

The normal form of all bacteria, described above, is called the **vegetative** form. Two groups of bacteria, the *Clostridia* and the *Bacilli* are capable of forming **spores**.

Spores are much smaller than the vegetative form and have a much thicker wall. They constitute a highly resistant stage occurring when certain essential nutrients are depleted. When conditions improve and the missing substances are again available, each spore germinates into a single bacterium again. It must be appreciated that spores are not eggs. The process is not a form of reproduction since one organism becomes one spore and reverts to one organism again.

Spores are particularly important in the context of sterilisation since they are extremely resistant to drying, heat and disinfectant chemicals.

The vegetative forms of bacteria are easily killed. To kill the highly resistant spores, much higher temperatures and more drastic chemicals are needed.

GROWTH AND REPRODUCTION

In suitable conditions, each bacterium increases to a critical size. The genetic material in the protoplast is then halved and a division develops across the cell by an ingrowth of the cell wall. The bacterium thus divides into two **daughter cells** and the process of growth and division is repeated.

The separation may be complete or the daughter cells may remain attached. Thus, following repeated division, pairs, chains or clumps of cells may be formed. The time from one cell-division to the next is called the **mean generation time**. It may be anything from 20 minutes to 24 hours depending on species and conditions.

When bacteria are introduced into a liquid culture medium (see page 7), for the first one to four hours there is considerable cell growth but little division. This is followed by a period of rapid cell division and a vast increase in cell numbers, with a levelling off after about 24 hours. Thereafter, following a few hours steady state, cells die more rapidly than new ones are produced. The number of cells declines and ultimately, after days or months, the culture becomes sterile.

GROWTH REQUIREMENTS

Water is essential for growth although organisms may be freeze-dried and stored in a vacuum. Even after long periods of freezing they may remain capable of regeneration. Several inorganic substances are necessary including some quite exotic ones which are needed for enzyme formation.

Some organisms, termed **autotrophs**, can live in an exclusively inorganic environment. The carbon and nitrogen for their proteins etc. can be obtained from carbon dioxide, ammonia, nitrates and nitrites. A few contain chlorophyll and are able to carry out photosynthesis in the same manner as plants. None of the autotrophs are important medically.

All medically significant bacteria are **heterotrophs**. They need organic material for growth and metabolism but the exact requirements differ from one species to another. Some organisms have very specific requirements for particular substances such as amino acids or vitamins.

All bacteria require carbon dioxide for growth but they often generate it themselves. Oxygen requirements vary. For some bacteria it is essential. These are termed **strict** or **obligate aerobes**. Others, known as **anaerobes** can grow only in the absence of oxygen. The majority, however, can grow either in its presence or absence. These are called **facultative anaerobes**.

Other environmental requirements include a suitable pH (see Appendix 2), usually 7.2 to 7.6. Growth of most medically important bacteria ceases outside the range pH 5.0 to 9.0.

Not surprisingly, bacteria which are capable of producing disease in humans (**pathogenic**) usually grow best at body temperature (37 °C). Non-pathogenic organisms, according to their preferred environment, may multiply at or below freezing point or up to 80 °C.

CLASSIFICATION OF BACTERIA

All plants and animals are classified and known scientifically by two names. The **genus** is the immediate group to which the plant or animal and its very close relatives belong. The **species** is the specific type within the genus. This two name classification, the **Linnaean** or **binomial** system, is also applied to bacteria.

As an example, for the organism *Escherichia coli*, *Escherichia* is the genus and *coli* the species. It is common to abbreviate the genus to one letter or syllable. Thus *Escherichia coli* becomes *E. coli*.

Bacteria are classified by various characteristics. These include their shape (morphology), the way in which they take up dyes when stained for microscopical examination, their nutritional and metabolic requirements (e.g. whether they are aerobic or anaerobic), etc.

As noted earlier, the bacteria are a very heterogeneous group placed together for convenience. As knowledge grows so more scientific methods of classification are applied.

CLASSIFICATION BY SHAPE

Three basic shapes of the bacterial cell are recognised – spherical (coccus), straight rod (bacillus) and curved or spiral rod (*Vibrio, Campylobacter, Spirillum, Spirochaete* etc.).

There are many varieties within each shape. Cocci occur in bunches (*Staphylococcus*); slightly pointed or oval and in chains (*Streptococcus*); in pairs (*Neisseria*), fours or eights etc.

The rods are usually clearly rod shaped but some rods such as *Brucella* and *Haemophilus* are short and rounded. These are termed *coccobacilli*.

As noted above, the word 'Bacillus' is used as a general term to describe straight rod-shaped organisms. Unfortunately it also has a second meaning being the name of a particular genus of rods. *B. anthracis* and *B. subtilis* are common examples. Other variants on the rod shape include club-shapes, threads and branching filaments.

The spiral rods vary. Some are just curved to form comma shapes (*Vibrio*). Others are long rigid rods with several curves (*Spirillum*) or long flexible spirals (*Spirochaetes*).

Bacteria are measured in micrometres (μm). A micrometre is one thousandth part of a millimetre or one millionth of a metre, 1×10^{-6} metres.

A red blood cell is about 7 μm in diameter and cocci are about 1 μm across. *Bacilli* range from 2.5 μm in length and 0.5 to 1 μm wide whilst *Spirochaetes* may range up to 25 μm in length.

CLASSIFICATION BY STAINING REACTIONS

There are two important staining techniques used to classify bacteria: **Gram's stain** and the **Ziehl-Neelsen stain**.

Bacteria are cultured on **nutrient media**. Where the medium is solid they form visible **colonies** – whitish or coloured spots, perhaps 1–3 mm in diameter – each of which arises from one bacterium. To examine and identify the organism microscopically, a small amount of the colony is spread on a microscope slide and 'fixed' by passing it over a flame. Solutions of various dyes can then be flooded over the slide and the excess washed off. Certain bacteria 'take up' (i.e. are coloured by) particular dyes. They can then be seen under the high power of a microscope as red or blue cocci or bacilli, for example.

Gram's staining method is a two-colour process involving the use of violet and red dyes. Organisms which are coloured violet in this method are termed Gram-positive (Gram+) whilst those coloured red are Gram-negative (Gram−). If a slide with both Gram-positive and Gram-negative organisms is stained in this way the violet or red organisms show up very clearly.

Although this method may seem arbitrary, Gram-positive and Gram-negative organisms do vary quite widely from one another and the method is useful in classification. A few organisms cannot be stained at all, or only with difficulty by Gram's stain.

The *Mycobacterium* species is one group which is difficult to stain by Gram's method. It can be stained by Ziehl–Neelsen's process, using a red dye followed by an acid wash and blue or green dye. Because they resist the acid wash, those organisms which retain the red dye are referred to as **acid-fast**.

There are several other staining techniques which are used to emphasise special features of some bacteria.

CULTURE OF BACTERIA

Bacteria can be cultured (grown) on various media.

Culturing is a normal part of the identification process. There may be relatively few organisms to be seen in whatever sample of material needs to be examined and there may be several different types present. Culturing vastly increases the numbers and suitable techniques enable the different types to be separated. There are then adequate numbers available for identification. The composition of the culture medium can be varied to encourage the growth of some types whilst suppressing others, again aiding identification.

The media used may be solid or liquid and they are basically meat soups. Other materials such as blood, serum, yeast extract, glucose, etc. may be added. Antibiotics may be used to suppress the growth of sensitive organisms and permit the growth of resistant ones. The solid media are basically the same as the liquid ones but are stiffened to a gel by adding a gelatin-like seaweed derivative called agar. Such gels remain firm at incubator temperatures (37 °C). Media, dishes, etc., are all sterilised before use.

The material being cultured (blood, faeces, water, etc.) is spread on to the medium and incubated at 37 °C. Each bacterium in the original smear will develop into a colony which is visible as a whitish or coloured spot on the plate. Some spots will be so close together as to be inseparable but others will be separate and identifiable. The colour, shape, etc. of each colony is important for identification. A little of each colony can then be spread on a slide. This is stained and examined microscopically. For anaerobic organisms the plates are incubated in an atmosphere of hydrogen and carbon dioxide.

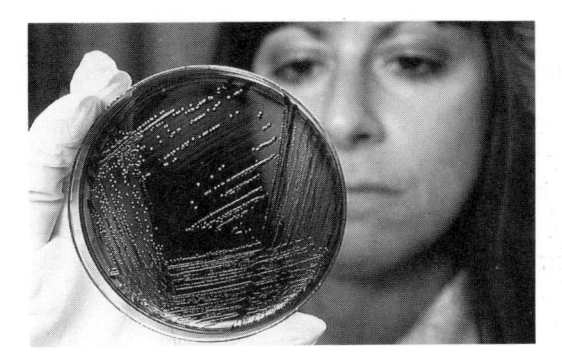

Technician examining colonies of Salmonella *growing on agar medium in a Petri dish. The lines of colonies follow the lines of the platinum wire loop with which the original material was spread on to the plate before incubation. Close examination will show that each line is made up of a row of tiny dots, each of which is a colony of many millions of organisms arising from just one in the original inoculum.*

Almost all bacteria can be grown in culture media (*Treponema pallidum*, the causative organism of syphilis, is an exception). In some cases, their ability to produce disease in experimental animals may need to be used for identification or isolation.

VIRULENCE

Pathogenic organisms possess varying degrees of **virulence** or ability to produce disease.

This depends on a number of factors, not all clearly understood. These include **invasiveness** – the ability to penetrate the host's defences and multiply – and **toxicity** – the ability to damage host tissues. To multiply, they need all those factors required for normal growth. Some may increase their chance of survival by resistance to the host's natural defence system. Many produce **toxins** – bacterial products which are directly harmful to host tissue cells.

There are two main groups of toxins: **exotoxins** and **endotoxins**.

Exotoxins are proteins and they are the most poisonous substances known. They diffuse from the bacteria into the surrounding medium. In the body, even in the absence of the bacteria themselves, they produce the typical effects of the disease concerned. Exotoxins are produced mainly by Gram-positive organisms such as *C. diphtheriae*, *Cl. tetani*, *Strep. pyogenes*, *Staph. aureus*, etc. A few Gram-negatives such as the *Shigella* species, *Vibrio cholera* etc. also produce them.

Endotoxins are an integral part of the bacterial cell and they are only liberated when the cell is broken down after death. They are less toxic than the exotoxins. They are produced by Gram-negative organisms including *Salmonella, Shigella, Brucella* etc. Some organisms produce both exotoxins and endotoxins.

ANTIGENS AND ANTIBODIES

As part of its defence mechanisms, the body produces **antibodies**. It is stimulated to do so by **antigens**.

Antigens are complex substances, often protein-like, produced amongst other things by bacteria. Antibodies react with antigens to neutralise them and the antibodies are usually specific for a particular antigen. When the body becomes **immune** to a disease, either by vaccination or other means it has developed antibodies to that disease. The antigen/antibody reaction is very important and will be discussed further in Chapter 3.

Exotoxins are highly antigenic – the host readily produces specific antibodies which neutralise them completely. They may be modified by heat and by chemicals such as formaldehyde when they lose their toxicity but retain antigenicity. These so-called **toxoids** are therefore capable of stimulating antibody production without producing disease. Toxoids are widely used for immunisation.

Endotoxins are only weakly antigenic and the intact organism is only partly neutralised by the host's antibodies. They cannot be converted into toxoids.

COMMON PATHOGENIC BACTERIA

This section summarises very briefly the commoner organisms which the student is likely to meet by name. The information given should be sufficient to familiarise the reader with the subject and some organisms will be mentioned again in later chapters. Where more information about specific organisms is required, a book on the appropriate branch of microbiology should be consulted. A list of such books is given in Chapter 10.

Most of the organisms discussed produce disease in humans. A few are normal inhabitants of the body, especially of the gut (gastro-intestinal tract). Others are found routinely in the respiratory tract, in the vagina or on the skin. These normal inhabitants which do not usually cause disease, are called **commensals**.

Before leaving bacteria it is convenient to mention a group of very small organisms which lie between bacteria and viruses in size and have some characteristics of both, although they are clearly bacteria. These are the *Rickettsiae* and *Coxiellae*, the *Chlamydiae* and the *Mycoplasmas*. *Rickettsiae* are the causative organisms of typhus, transmitted by lice. *Chlamydiae* are associated with trachoma, a severe tropical eye disease, and with psittacosis, a disease of birds transmissible to humans causing a severe pneumonia. *Mycoplasma pneumoniae* is the commonest cause of non-bacterial pneumonia in humans.

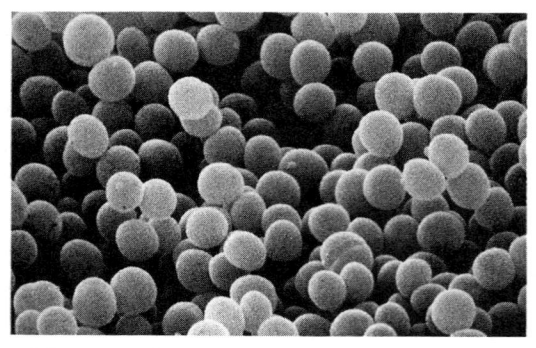

Staph. aureus. *Photograph taken by a scanning electron microscope × about 8000. Note the round shape of the organism (coccus) and the way it occurs in clumps characteristic of* Staphylococci.

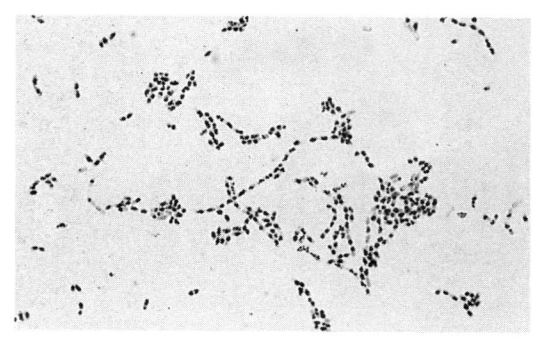

Bacillus cereus. *This is a light micrograph × 500. Note the rod shape of the organisms compared with the spheres of* Staphylococcus.

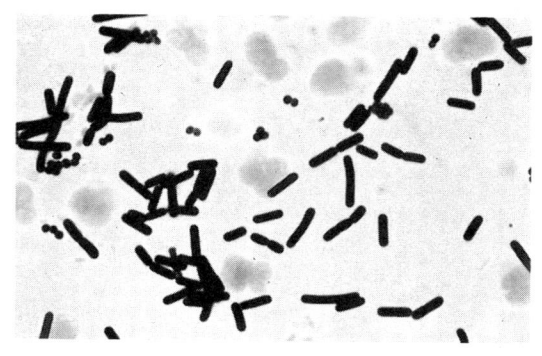

Clostridium perfringens. *Micrograph of a pus smear from wound infected with* Cl. perfringens. *The small rods are the bacilli and the larger round objects are cell debris in the pus, probably dead white blood cells.*

Group/Genus/Species	Characteristics and other names	Diseases caused/relevance to readers' work
Gram-positive Cocci		
Staphylococcus	Clumps of globular cocci.	
Staph. aureus (See opposite.)	Commensal in respiratory tract.	Acute skin infections, boils, carbuncles, pustules, impetigo. Spread by coughing, sneezing, or in wound exudates. Common cause of food poisoning.
Streptococcus	Chains of globular cocci.	
Strep. pyogenes		Tonsillitis, wound infections, often in association with Staph. aureus.
Strep. pneumoniae	Capsulated, occurring in pairs (Diplococcus). Normally present in throat. Also known as Pneumococcus.	75 per cent of bacterial pneumonias caused by this organism.
Gram-negative Cocci		
Neisseria	Aerobic, occurring in small clusters. Several species are commensals.	
N. gonorrhoeae	Gonococcus.	Gonorrhoea.
N. meningitides	Meningococcus.	One form of meningitis.
Gram-positive Bacilli		
Bacillus	This is the genus Bacillus. Aerobic, spore-forming rods.	
B. anthracis	Anthrax Bacillus.	Anthrax, a disease of animals communicable to humans. Both a skin disease and a serious, potentially fatal pneumonia.
B. cereus (See opposite.)	Occurs in cereals, spices and especially in rice.	Storage of infected food in a warm place produces a toxin which causes food poisoning when consumed.

Group/Genus/Species	Characteristics and other names	Diseases caused/relevance to readers' work
B. subtilis	Produces very resistant spores, used to test the effectiveness of sterilisers (see Chapter 5).	Not pathogenic.
Clostridium	Anaerobic, spore-forming rods. Found in soil and decomposing animal matter. May occur as commensals in gut.	
Cl. tetani		Tetanus.
Cl. botulinum		Botulism, a particularly dangerous and commonly fatal form of food poisoning.
Cl. oedematiens		Gas gangrene.
Cl. septicum		Gas gangrene.
Cl. perfringens (See page 10.)	Cl. welchii. Common in gut of humans and animals and in soil.	Second most important cause of food poisoning in the UK. Spread on infected meat by insects and hands of careless food operatives
Corynebacterium	Fine, non-spore-forming rods, non-motile and non-capsulated. Several non-pathogenic species are common commensals known as 'diptheroids'.	
C. diphtheriae		Diphtheria.
Mycobacterium	Acid-fast, strictly aerobic rods. Non-motile, non-spore-forming. Difficult to stain by Gram's process.	
M. tuberculosis	Tubercle bacillus.	Main cause of tuberculosis in humans.

Group/Genus/Species	Characteristics and other names	Diseases caused/relevance to readers' work
M. bovis		Tuberculosis in cattle.
M. leprae		Leprosy.
Actinomyces, Nocardia and Micropolyspora	These genera occur as branching filaments.	Occasionally pathogenic in humans.
Streptomyces	Filamentous organisms. An important source of antibiotics (e.g. streptomycin).	Non-pathogenic.
Lactobacillus		
L. acidophillus	A normal inhabitant of the vagina.	
Erysipelothrix and Listeria	Two similar genera.	Pathogenic in animals and occasionally in humans.
Gram-negative Bacilli	Conveniently divisible into two groups, **enterobacteria** and **parvobacteria**.	
Enterobacteria	A large group also known as intestinal bacilli or **coliforms**.	
E. coli	Many types. Primarily a commensal in the gut.	Pathogenic in urinary tract infections, appendicitis, peritonitis, wound infections and infantile gastroenteritis. Its presence in water is often taken as an indication of faecal contamination.
Klebsiella	Occasional respiratory commensal.	Can cause a rare and serious form of pneumonia.
Salmonella	Motile rods, parasitic in gut of humans, other animals and birds.	Salmonella species are very common on raw meats and especially on the lining of the inner cavity of poultry prepared for sale. Domestic pets, vermin, insects etc. may spread it around food preparation areas. Often borne by symptomless carriers (see Chapter 3).

Group/Genus/Species	Characteristics and other names	Diseases caused/relevance to readers' work
S. typhimurium		The commonest cause of salmonella food poisoning (salmonellosis) in humans.
S. typhi		Typhoid.
S. paratyphi A and B		Paratyphoid.
Shigella	Non-motile rods, parasitic in the gut.	Bacillary dysentery.
S. dysenteriae, S. boydi, S. flexneri and S. sonnei are the common species		
Proteus	Motile bacilli which change shape from near cocci to long filaments.	
Pseudomonas, Vibrio and Yersinia	Not coliforms but conveniently considered here.	
Ps. pyocyanea	Ps. aeruginosa	Commonly infects burns, wounds and ulcers and can cause severe urinary tract infections.
Vibrio cholerae	Comma-shaped rods, with flagella.	Cholera.
Y. pestis		Plague
Parvobacteria	A miscellaneous group of small bacteria, difficult to culture and nutritionally exacting.	
Pasteurella and Francisella		Primarily animal pathogens occasionally infecting humans.
Brucella		
B. abortus		Infects cows and humans, being the commonest cause of brucellosis in humans.
Haemophilus and Bordetella	Minute aerobic coccobacilli.	

Group/Genus/Species	Characteristics and other names	Diseases caused/relevance to readers' work
H. Influenzae	Human respiratory tract commensal.	Influenza is a viral infection (see page 23). *H. influenzae* often causes secondary infection in those with viral influenza. Also causes a dangerous meningitis in children.
B. pertussis		Whooping cough
Moraxella, Streptobacillus, Spirillum, Bacteroides, Fusobacterium, Bartonella Campylobacter and Calymmatobacterium		All are occasionally associated with human disease.
Legionella		
L. pneumophila		Legionnaires' disease, a severe respiratory infection, first recognised in 1976.
Spirochaetes	Motile spiral organisms, difficult to stain*.	Three genera are pathogenic.
Borrelia		
B. vincentii		Infections of throat and mouth.
Leptospira		Various species occur in animals, especially in rodents and are transmitted to man causing leptospirosis, Weil's disease.
Treponema		
T. pallidum		Syphilis, an exclusively human disease.

*Since the *Spirochaetes* (especially *T. pallidum*) are difficult to stain, they are normally examined microscopically by the dark field technique. In normal microscopic examination, light is reflected through the slide being examined. In the dark field technique, illumination is from the sides. Unstained organisms, almost invisible in direct light, then appear bright and silvery against an almost black background, somewhat like stars on a clear night.

CHAPTER 2

Viruses and other pathogenic organisms

Viruses are minute infective particles which are completely inactive outside the living cells which they infect. They have no metabolism nor do they reproduce except in such cells. They are clearly very near to the boundary between the living and the inanimate. In suitable environments they do behave as living organisms and are capable of reproduction and mutation. These are described below.

For the purposes of this book such terms as 'living', 'dead' and 'killed', will be used for convenience in discussing viruses.

CLASSIFICATION OF VIRUSES

No simple binomial system of classification has been devised for viruses.

They all contain nucleic acids, either **RNA** (ribonucleic acid) or **DNA** (deoxyribonucleic acid). On this basis they are classified as RNA or DNA viruses. A few are associated both with RNA and DNA and are known as RNA/DNA viruses. RNA is similar to DNA but has only a single chain of amino acids.

Further classification is based mainly on shape or structure and the viruses are named after the diseases which they produce. The virus of hepatitis B, for example, is referred to as HBV (hepatitis B virus). The AIDS virus is now known as HIV (human immunodeficiency virus). Names, subdivisions and diseases are discussed later in the chapter.

Certain viruses infect bacteria. They are known as **bacteriophages**.

STRUCTURE AND MORPHOLOGY

Viruses are too small to be seen under the optical microscope. Most information about them is derived from electron microscopy for which special techniques have been developed. They are measured in nanometres (nm), one nanometre is one thousandth of a micrometre, 1×10^{-9} metres.

Viruses range in size between about 20 and 300 nm. The smallest is thus only about one fiftieth and the largest about one third the diameter of an average coccus such as *staphylococcus*.

Viruses which infect animals (including humans) are roughly spherical in shape, although many have a number of regular flat faces. This shape is called a **polyhedron**.

Each individual virus particle is termed a **virion**. The virions comprise an inner core of DNA or RNA which may be a single molecule. This is surrounded by a protein case called a **capsid**. In addition some species have a further outer coat known as an **envelope**. This consists of fat and protein. It is derived from the wall of the host-cell in which the virion developed. In some cases this envelope may be responsible for the virion's infectivity. Some viruses have other basic shapes such as filaments whilst the largest may have a somewhat more complex structure.

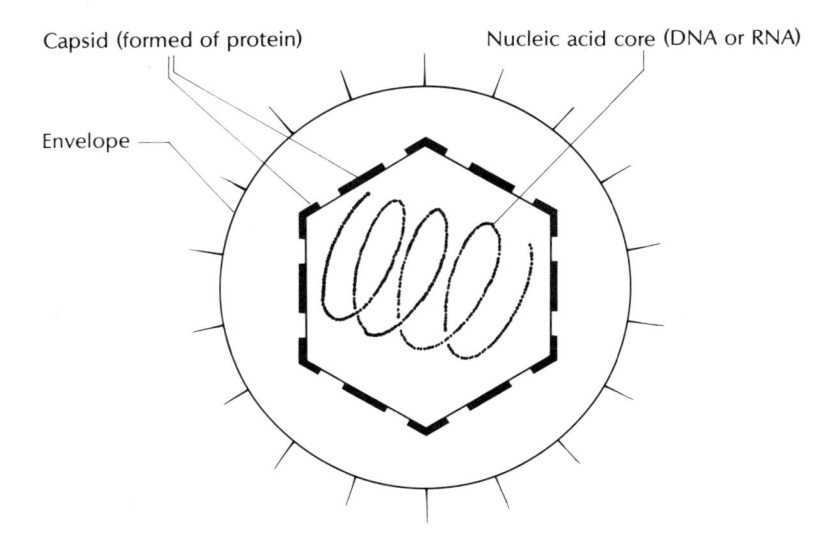

Structure of a virion.

INVASION OF HOST CELLS

Outside the cells of the infected host, virions are inactive, they neither reproduce nor metabolise. The nucleic acid is their essential component.

When the virus enters the host cell it uses that cell's mechanisms to reproduce itself. Its nucleic acid is replicated, that is exact copies or replicas are produced. New virus particles are assembled within the cell and usually the cell dies. The new particles are shed at or before death. Some viruses produce other effects on infected cells. The virus may, for instance, render the cell **malignant** and capable of producing **tumours**.

During the process of viral reproduction within the cell, the host whose cells are infected shows no sign of disease. This is the incubation period of viral infections.

After several cycles of cell infection, release of new virus particles and infection of further host cells, typical signs and symptoms of the disease appear. Recovery from virus disease is mainly the result of the activity of the host's **cell-mediated defences** (see Chapter 3).

All viruses are antigenic. Infected animals produce specific antibodies which may combine with the viral antigens. This renders the virus non-infective.

Unlike bacteria, viruses do not produce toxins. Their toxic effects are, in most cases, a function of the intact virion. A few, however, do seem to induce the production of a toxic substance.

Typical viral replication:
1. Virion approaches host cell to be infected.
2. Virion attaches to receptors on the cell wall.
3. Virion enters the cell.
4. Intact virion within cell.
5. Virion coat disintegrates exposing nucleic acid core.
6. This stage is known as eclipse. The virus is now present in the cell only as small non-infective sub-units which multiply within the cell.
7. Multiplying sub-units collecting within the infected cell.
8. Sub-units are assembled into new virions.
9. Cell dies and disintegrates. New virions are released.

Virion

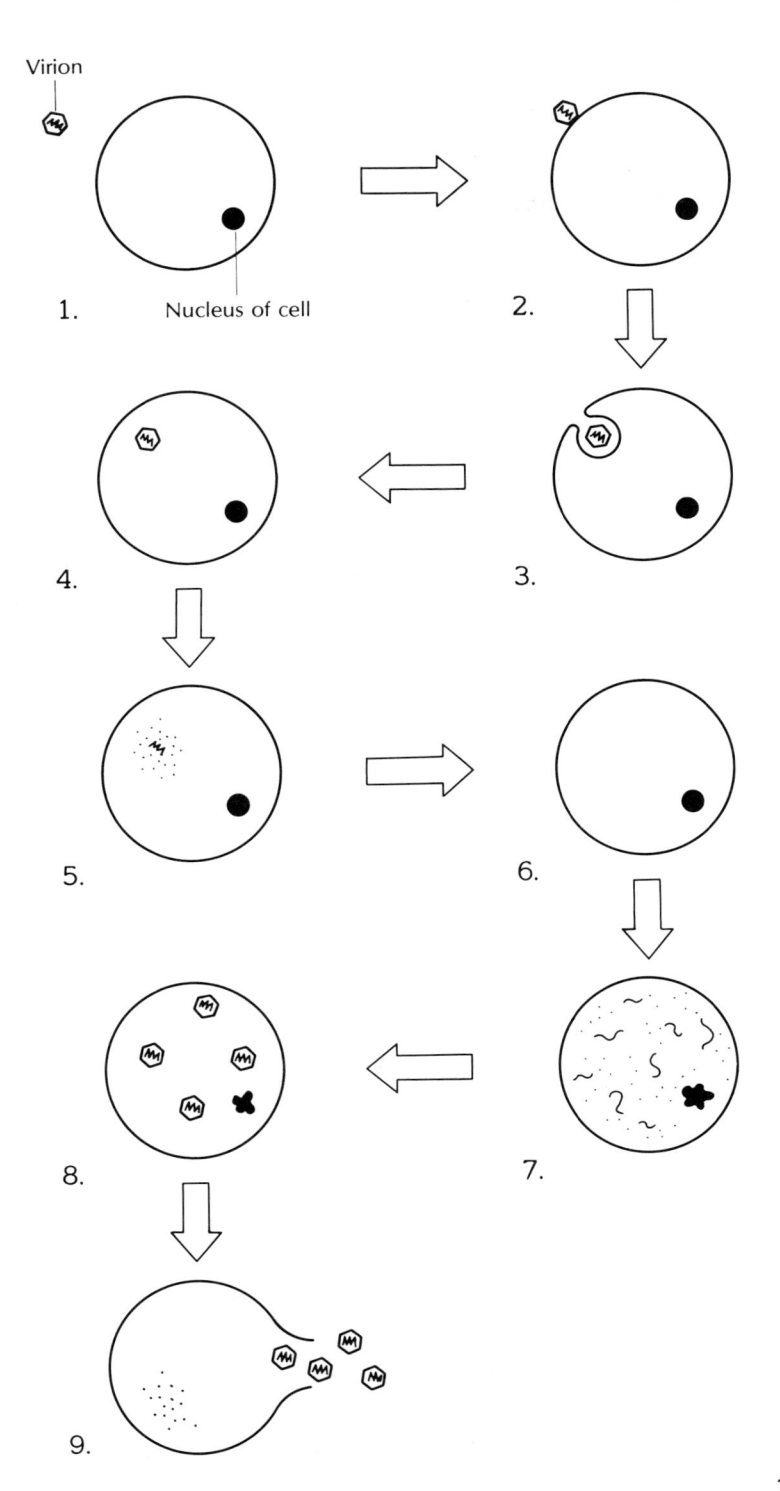

1. Nucleus of cell

2.

3.

4.

5.

6.

7.

8.

9.

Animal cells may respond to viral invasion by producing substances called **interferons** which interfere with the viral replication process.

Finally, viruses readily produce variations by mutation in which changes in the viral nucleic acid occurs. This results in a change in the characteristics of the virus.

In some cases the specific antigenicity is retained whilst virulence is reduced. This produces strains which can be used for inoculation against the disease. Yellow fever vaccine, for example, is produced in this way. In other cases a change in antigenicity occurs but virulence is retained. When this happens there will be little naturally acquired immunity in the population towards the infection so that an explosive outbreak of the disease can occur. This happened with Asian-type influenza in the late 1950s.

CULTURE OF VIRUSES

Unlike bacteria, viruses cannot be cultured on ordinary culture media. They can only be cultured in living tissue and special techniques must be used. Three methods are available using either intact animals, developing chick embryos in fertile hen eggs or **tissue-cultures**.

The study and identification of viruses and the diseases which they cause are much more difficult than with bacterial infections. This is especially true where live animals are the only culture medium in which the virus will reproduce. In the case of some human diseases the virus is so species-specific that only other primates, or even man himself, can be used. For example, information about the susceptibility of hepatitis B virus to various sterilising methods has been obtained by the use of chimpanzees (see Chapter 3). Intra-nasal inoculation of human volunteers has been used in the investigation of the common cold.

Many different types of virus will grow in developing hen-egg embryos. Hen eggs are normally sterile and are alive, cheap and easy to use. Windows may be cut in the shell for inoculation and observation. The egg and embryo contain various different tissues which can be used for virus culture. Smallpox, herpes, influenza and mumps viruses may all be grown in this way. Some viruses produce characteristic 'pocks' or spots on egg-tissues which are visible to the naked eye.

Many animal tissues will reproduce and grow, often in a characteristic way, on suitable culture media. These are called **tissue-cultures**. The animal tissues grown in this way are obtained from various sources, such as foetuses and associated tissues or malignancies and ordinary cells removed during surgery from humans, other primates or animals. Many viruses grow readily on such tissue-cultures.

IDENTIFICATION OF VIRUSES IN DISEASE CONDITIONS

This can be difficult due to the nature of viruses, as described above. Some virus particles in clinical specimens can be seen by electron microscopy. Viral antigens and their antibodies may be detected in the serum of an infected person.

Many adults carry antibodies against common viruses acquired during a lifetime of exposure and infection. Thus the presence of antibody alone may not indicate active infection. Where a virus is isolated, especially from blood or cerebrospinal fluid, and a concurrent increase in antibody levels to it is seen, this constitutes highly significant evidence of the existence of the viral infection.

IMPORTANT PATHOGENIC VIRUSES

Even to mention all the important viruses is beyond the scope of this book. Only a few important types can be discussed to illustrate the subject. These are shown in the table on pages 22-3 and the basic divisions of DNA and RNA viruses are used.

The names of groups of viruses are related to some property of the virus. As an example, arboviruses are borne by insects hence the name *arthropod-borne* – arbovirus. Other examples are shown in the table.

The shape of some viruses is described as icosahedral. An icosahedron is a regular body with 20 sides, each of which is an equilateral triangle.

As in the case of bacteria, interested readers requiring more information are referred to textbooks on microbiology (see Chapter 10).

Type and Group	Characteristics and comments	Diseases caused
DNA viruses		
Poxviruses	Large size, up to 300 nm in diameter. Grow readily in chick embryos and on tissue cultures.	Smallpox, and numerous animal diseases.
Herpesviruses	Icosahedral, up to 180 nm diameter. Readily cultured on chick embryos and tissue cultures. More common in humans than any other virus.	
Herpes simplex virus	Type 1, found in upper part of body. Type 2, much less common, found in lower part of body.	Herpes simplex (cold sores). Genital herpes affecting vagina, penis, vulva & cervix; transmitted sexually. Also causes neonatal herpes infections.
Herpes zoster virus		Herpes zoster (shingles) and chickenpox.
Cytomegalovirus		An important cause of opportunistic infections in AIDS patients.
Adenoviruses	Very common cause of human disease.	Respiratory disease such as pneumonias. Also meningitis and some eye infections.
Papovaviruses	Very small, up to 50 nm diameter. Icosahedral and non-enveloped.	Cause many human warts.
RNA viruses		
Picornaviruses	Named from 'pico' meaning very small and 'rna' from their RNA content. Icosahedral, non-enveloped, 20–30 nm in diameter. Inhabit gut and respiratory tract.	Polio, common colds and foot and mouth disease.

Type and Group	Characteristics and comments	Diseases caused
Rotaviruses		Infantile gastro-enteritis. Very frequent cause of death in infants especially in under-developed countries.
Orthomyxoviruses	Enveloped and may be spheroidal or filament-shaped.	Influenza in humans and some animals.
Paramyxoviruses	Commonly inhabit the respiratory tract.	Mumps, measles and severe respiratory diseases in young children.
Togaviruses		Yellow fever and many other tropical diseases. Also rubella (German measles).
RNA-DNA viruses	Helical shape and enveloped. Contain **reverse transcriptase**, an enzyme which plays a vital part in its replication. Detection of this enzyme is important in the recognition of infection by the virus and it is the target for drug therapy.	Associated with certain tumours.
HIV	Human immunodeficiency virus.	HIV infections and AIDS.
Miscellaneous Viruses	Important to readers are those causing hepatitis (see Chapter 3).	
HAV	A small, non-enveloped icosahedral RNA virus.	Hepatitis A
HBV	An enveloped DNA virus about 40 nm in diameter.	Hepatitis B

OTHER PATHOGENIC ORGANISMS

Apart from bacteria and viruses, a number of other organisms cause infections in humans. They include the Fungi, Protista, Helminths or Worms and certain arthropods. Works on microbiology and medical entomology will provide more detailed information. Readers will normally be interested in only one or two of these. They will, however, have little difficulty in picking out those which are applicable to their own profession.

FUNGI

There are three main types of fungi, the **yeasts** and **yeast-like fungi**, the **filamentous fungi** and the **dimorphic fungi**.

The yeasts are round or oval bodies which reproduce by budding. Whilst generalised infections caused by them are rare the condition cryptococcosis may occur in severe immunodepression, infecting the lungs, skin and other organs. The yeast-like fungi normally occur as yeasts but they can form chains or filaments of elongated cells which reproduce by budding off yeast-like cells. Well-known members of this group are *Candida albicans* and *Malassezia furfur*.

Candida is a common inhabitant of the human mouth and throat where it causes thrush. It is also a common cause of vaginitis – vaginal inflammation. In some patients with deficient cell-mediated immunity (see Chapter 3) it may cause an intractable infection of the skin and nails as well as of the mouth. Generalised infections, as of the lungs, can also occur.

M. furfur is the causitive organism of pityriasis versicolor (also known as tinea versicolor), a common scaly skin infection.

Filamentous fungi, as the name suggests, grow in filaments which reproduce by forming spores. This is a true reproductive process and the spores must be distinguished from bacterial spores considered in Chapter 1. The filaments tend to form tangled masses known as **mycelium**. Of particular interest to those working on skin and hair are the **dermatophytes** – fungi affecting the keratin of body surfaces causing the conditions tinea and ringworm.

Members of the genus *Microsporum* cause ringworm of hair and skin and include *M. audouini* (tinea capitis in children), and *M. canis* (ringworm in cats and dogs, which spreads to children).

The second genus in the dermatophyte group is *Trichophyton* whose species attack skin, hair and nails. Tinea pedis (athlete's foot) is caused by *T. interdigitale* which affects more than 50 per cent of the population, whilst the chronic scalp infection favus is caused by *T. schoenleini*. Severe skin and nail infections are caused by *T. rubrum* whilst *T. sulphureum (T. tonsurans)* and *T. violaceum* also cause disease in humans. Other species attack animals such as horses and cattle.

Of the third genus in the group – *Epidermophyton* – only one species is important in human medicine. This is *E. floccosum*, attacking skin and nails but not hair. It is the most frequent cause of tinea cruris (ringworm of the groin).

Apart from the dermatophytes, several other filamentous fungi are important in causing human infections. *Aspergillus* is a very common genus whose species are involved in lung and ear disease. Of some importance in the catering industry, especially in the third world countries, is *A. flavus*. When grown in certain foodstuffs, ground nuts have been implicated, a substance called **aflatoxin** is produced. This is a potent liver poison and is also carcinogenic. It is thought to be responsible for some cases of liver cancer and cirrhosis of the liver in India.

Fungal infections are in many cases kept in check by competition from bacteria. When bacterial populations are suppressed, for example in treatment by broad-spectrum antibiotics, fungal infections which are immune to antibiotics, tend to proliferate. The normally harmless **saprophytes** (organisms which live on dead organic matter) of the genera *Mucor* and *Rhizopus* may be involved in fatal lung and brain infections in these circumstances.

It is interesting to note that some members of the saprophytic genus *Penicillium* produce the antibiotic penicillin.

The **dimorphic** fungi (dimorphic means 'two forms') have a filamentous form when growing as saprophytes at lower temperatures and a yeast phase at body temperature when parasitic. Diseases caused by members of this group are common in Africa and the Americas but extremely rare in the UK.

Apart from the situations mentioned above, fungi are particularly important in the food industry where they are responsible for much food deterioriation. Most food is essentially organic matter and is an excellent basis for the growth of saprophytic fungi.

PROTISTA

These are unicellular organisms associated with several human diseases.

They cause tropical conditions such as malaria, trypanosomiasis, etc. Amoebae belong to this group and cause amoebic dysentery. *Trichomonas vaginalis* is an important inhabitant of the vagina where it may cause disease. *Pneumocystis carinii* is found in the respiratory tract. It causes one of the most important opportunistic infections associated with AIDS: *P. carinii* pneumonia (see Chapter 3).

HELMINTHS OR WORMS

These vary from the small worms which are common causes of tropical disease to intestinal worms such as tapeworms, roundworms or threadworms. They are of considerable medical importance, and some health care workers may meet the conditions caused by them. Since they are, for the most part transmitted by food, they are of particular interest in the food industries.

In the UK, only three species of worms are commonly encountered and these are described below. The first two belong to the group Nematodes which are round non-segmented worms, often tapered at both ends.

Threadworms (*Enterobius vermicularis*) are extremely common in all parts of the world. Health-care workers dealing with family situations will meet them frequently. Threadworms look like small white wriggling threads about 1 cm in length. They inhabit the small intestine and are often passed in the stools. The female emerges from the anus at night and lays her eggs. These cause intense itching and in scratching the eggs are transferred to the fingers and ultimately to the mouth. They are swallowed and hatch into a further generation. Usually all members of a family become affected and all should be treated at the same time. Threadworms spread rapidly amongst groups of children via infected hands and dust.

Roundworms (*Ascaris lumbricoides*) are much larger and up to 30 cm in length. The adults look like pale earthworms. They inhabit the intestinal tract, usually in pairs. Fertile eggs, passed with the faeces, infect soil, and food contaminated by them may be consumed. They hatch into larvae in the duodenum and find their way via the blood to the lungs. Here they develop and then ascend into the back of the throat when they are swallowed to mature in the gut into adult worms.

Several other nematodes whose preferred hosts are dogs, pigs, rats and other animals (*Toxocara, Trichinella, Trichuris*, etc.) may also affect humans. The general route of infection is either by eating meat from infected animals or by consuming food contaminated by faecally infected soil. These infections are much commoner in underdeveloped countries where sanitary conditions are primitive and human excreta may be used as fertiliser for food crops.

The third worm common in the UK is *Taenia saginata*, the beef tapeworm. This belongs to the group of flat worms known as

Platyhelminthes. A characteristic of these worms is that they alternate between two hosts, in this case, humans and cattle. The head of a tapeworm is about the size of a large pinhead and is attached to the intestinal wall. From it progressively larger flat segments develop so that the adult is a flat worm up to about 10 cm long. The ultimate segments, which are little more than packets of eggs, detach themselves and are passed in the faeces. The eggs are picked up by grazing cattle, hatch in the gut and migrate to the muscles where they form cysts. If this affected meat is inadequately cooked and eaten by a human, adult worms develop, attach themselves to the gut wall and the cycle is repeated.

Less common is the pork tapeworm, *T. solium* which alternates similarly between man and the pig. This is a much larger worm and may attain five metres in length. Here, the larval stage which normally occurs in the pig, may develop in man, causing the disease known as cysticercosis. The larvae become encysted in the muscles and may do so in the brain, causing epilepsy. (Most cases of epilepsy, of course, arise from other causes.)

A third tapeworm (*Diphyllobothrium latum*) results from eating raw or undercooked infected fish. It is common in fish-eating areas of Scandinavia, Iceland and the USA.

Many other worm infections occur in various parts of the world. Cleanliness in washing and handling food, and adequate cooking are important aspects in preventing the spread of many of them, as is the avoidance of vectors such as dogs, rats, etc. in food preparation areas.

ARTHROPOD INFECTIONS

The arthropods are the largest phylum or group in the animal kingdom. They include insects, crustacea, arachnids and many others.

They are associated with human infection in two basic ways. Firstly they act as **vectors** (carriers or spreaders) of the causative organisms of many diseases. These are considered in more detail in the next chapter. Secondly some arthropods actually infect the human body themselves. These also may spread disease and will be considered now.

The commonest arthropod invaders which are important to readers are **lice** and the **scabies** mite.

There are three lice infecting man: *Pthirus pubis*, the pubic or crab louse; *Pediculus humanus humanus (P. corporis)*, the body louse; *Pediculus humanus capitis*, the head louse. All feed by sucking the blood of the host and in doing so may spread disease.

Both body and head lice have a very similar life cycle. Infection occurs by close contact between donor and recipient of infection, by heads touching frequently, by sharing beds or in crowded conditions such as prisons. The female lays eggs which are attached to the base of hairs and are known as **nits**. They hatch in seven to ten days, the empty nit remaining firmly attached to the hair, and the newly hatched **nymphs** attain adulthood in about seven to nine days. In head infections only about 10 to 20 lice are normally found. Severe infections in which the hair becomes matted with lice, nits and exudate from pustules from infected bites can occur. Both bacteria and fungi may infect the bites. Length of hair is not important so far as infection rates are concerned but women and children are much more frequently infected by head lice than men.

Apart from the above infections, body lice are associated with the spread of rickettsiae such as typhus and spirochaete infections.

Pubic lice are usually spread at sexual intercourse.

Scabies is caused by the scabies mite, a small insect, *Sarcoptes scabiei*. These mites are not normally vectors of disease but they eat their way into the **stratum corneum** – the surface layers of the skin. This produces intense itching and scratching commonly with secondary infection. As with lice infections, it is spread by close association such as bed-sharing.

CHAPTER 3

Infection and disease

Infection is defined as 'the introduction of pathogenic organisms into or on to the body of a host'. Specifically it refers to micro-organisms such as bacteria, rickettsiae, viruses, protists or fungi.

This chapter describes how bacteria and viruses invade the body and cause disease. The body's reaction to infection is discussed. Hepatitis B and AIDS are conditions of particular concern and these are considered in more detail.

SOURCES OF INFECTION

Although infecting organisms can originate from several sources, they normally come from one of the following:

- humans
- animals
- inanimate objects.

HUMAN SOURCES

Human beings are the most likely source of infection. This is because organisms tend to adapt to a particular host. Thus an organism which infects one human will probably readily infect another.

The transfer of infection from one person to another is called **cross-infection**. It is essential to avoid cross-infection between clients. Indeed the whole object of this book is to make the reader aware of the risks and provide the knowledge with which to avoid them.

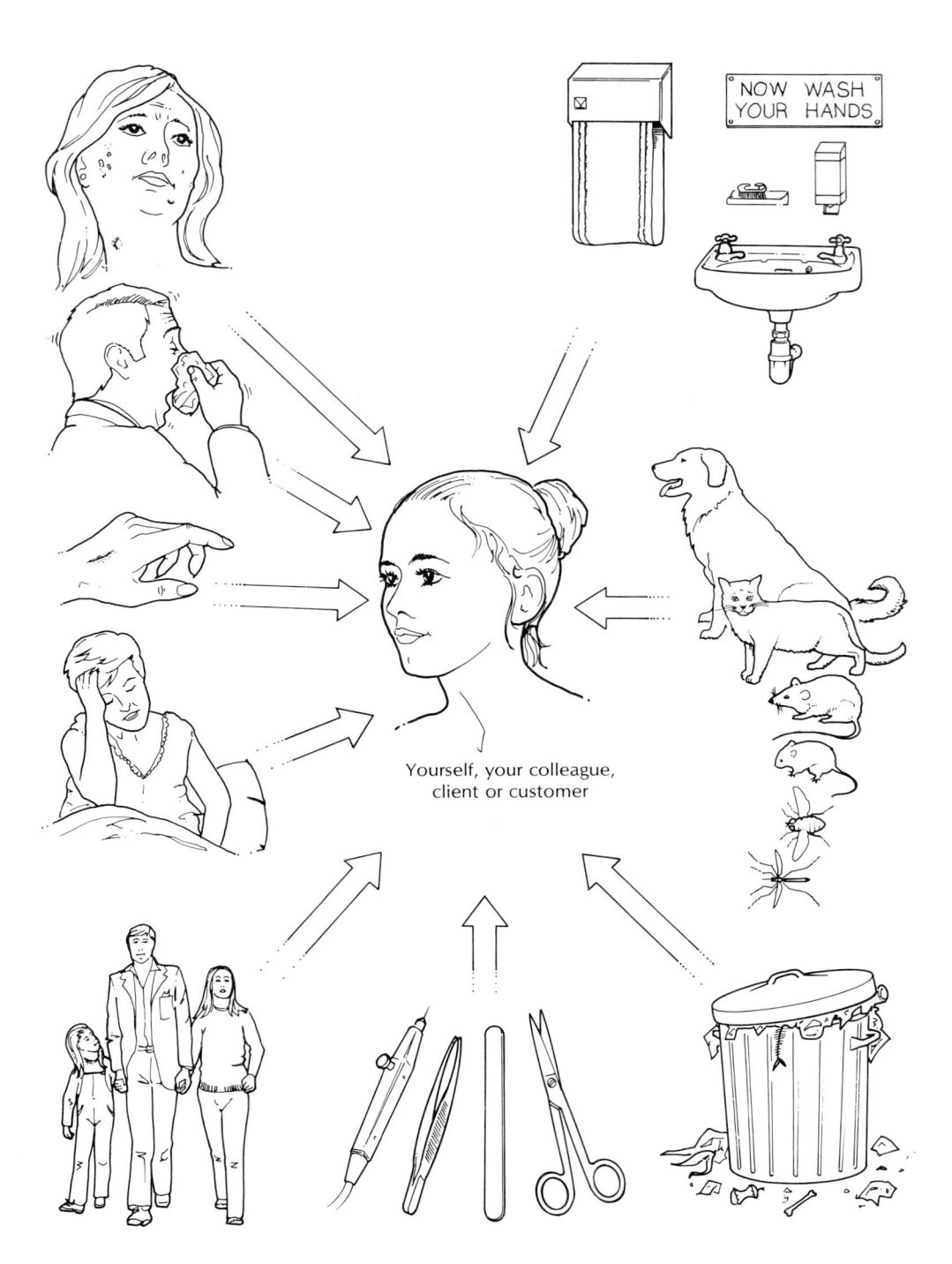

Potential sources of infection.

The commonest source of human infection in beauty and health care is the client. Many potentially pathogenic organisms live on or in the human body as commensals, without causing disease. In certain circumstances they may assume their pathogenic role.

Vast numbers of commensals live harmlessly in the gut and play an important part in waste disposal. Some of these, for example *E. coli*, may, if they escape into the abdominal cavity, cause peritonitis. Others inhabit the upper respiratory tract quite harmlessly. In virus infections, or conditions in which immunosuppression has occurred, invasion by commensals may take place. Thus in influenza, secondary infection by bacteria may result in pneumonia whilst examples of opportunistic infections following immunosuppression in AIDS patients will be discussed later in this chapter.

People with active diseases are an obvious source of infection. Respiratory infections such as colds, influenza, etc., are spread by the patient coughing or exhaling droplets of sputum containing pathogenic organisms. Sores, abscesses, ulcers, and infected wounds, are all potent sources of pathogens. These are easily transmitted to others via small wounds. Such wounds can be caused during beauty therapy or in health care. On the other hand, the diseases from which a client is suffering may be deep-seated with no outward communication in which case simple cross infection is unlikely.

Faeces and, in disease, urine will also contain pathogens.

Three other groups of humans are common sources of infection.

Firstly, those who are infected and 'incubating' disease. Although they appear quite healthy, active disease will develop and such persons are often highly infectious.

Secondly there are those who have had a disease and are recovering from it. They may or may not be infectious, depending on the condition and the stage of recovery.

The symptomless carriers form the third group. These are persons who may never have knowingly suffered from the disease but the organisms exist in them as commensals. Often these commensals inhabit the gut, in which case the carrier tends to excrete them in his faeces. Such persons may be careless in personal hygiene. If they are handling food which is not subsequently cooked, they become responsible for outbreaks of such conditions as *Salmonella* food poisoning. On the other hand, the conditions which they carry may be caused by blood-borne viruses. Skin-piercing cosmetic operations such as ear-piercing or electrolysis may then carry the infection from one person to another.

Clearly the first and third of these groups are most important. The carrier state is unlikely to be apparent unless investigated, and carriers are usually totally unaware that they could spread disease.

ANIMAL SOURCES OF INFECTION

These are less important, but are still responsible for the spread of a number of important conditions, especially in the tropics and in underdeveloped countries.

In some cases the organism needs two hosts and its life-cycle depends on an alternation between these. Tapeworms, alternating between the pig and humans are a typical example. Malaria, alternating between a particular species of mosquito and humans is another. In other cases, organisms are merely transferred from animals to humans. In tuberculosis and brucellosis, cattle are the animal source and untreated milk carries the disease to humans.

INANIMATE OBJECTS

Various pathogens, especially Gram-negative spore-forming bacteria, are found in dust, soil, decaying animal and vegetable matter, and untreated water. Any of these can carry the disease to a receptive host.

ROUTES OF INFECTION

There are three main entry points for disease into a new host (apart from transfer of disease from the mother to her unborn child across the placenta – syphilis and rubella may spread in this manner). These are:
- via the respiratory tract – nose, nasal passages, trachea, bronchi and lungs
- via the alimentary tract – mouth, oesophagus, stomach and gut
- through the skin and other surfaces.

Some organisms gain access by more than one route.

Via the respiratory tract
Airborne material such as dust and especially contaminated droplets from the coughs of infected persons enter by this route. It is particularly important for viral conditions such as the common cold and influenza.

When working on the faces of clients, if either client or operator has an upper respiratory infection, it is wise to wear a surgical mask. These are available quite cheaply from suppliers of surgical goods, and give protection to both parties.

Via the alimentary tract
Organisms may enter a host in infected foods contaminated by food-handlers who are carriers.

The risk is minimized if people always wash their hands after using the toilet, changing nappies, etc. Workers with open skin infections not protected by dressings can contaminate food. Coughing by food-handlers may infect foods with droplets of saliva or particles of pus from respiratory infections. Flies and cockroaches may transfer infection to food from their feet or by vomiting infected material. Both feed indiscriminately on faecal matter and food materials. It is imperative that they be excluded from food preparation and storage areas.

Water may be contaminated by sewage especially in hot or underdeveloped countries. Conditions such as hepatitis A and poliomyelitis are spread in this way.

Through the skin or other surfaces
This route is important to beauty professionals whose work is primarily concerned with skin and hair.

Infected equipment, even if it does not penetrate the skin, can spread such infections as impetigo, boils, warts, herpes simplex etc. Towels, swabs and dressings are also implicated. Where there are slight wounds or skin abrasions, organisms such as *Streptococci* and *Staphylococci* may be introduced.

More important for many readers is the **injection** or **parenteral** route.

Electrolysists, ear-piercers, acupuncturists, tattooists and others concerned with introducing needles into the skin can cause cross infection. Hepatitis B and other diseases are known to have been spread in this way. Although not yet an important route for the spread of AIDS, it could become so.

Cross infection by hair electrolysis is rare, but workers in this field should always take adequate precautions. Comedone extractors and accidental injury by hairdresser's scissors and razors are other cosmetic risks. Chiropody and manicure instruments may also cause small wounds.

Sexual contact is an important surface route by which disease is spread.

Sex-related infections such as gonorrhoea and syphilis have now been joined by HIV infection. Hepatitis B and herpes simplex may also be spread in this way as are many less familiar diseases.

A final source of infection by skin-inoculation is from insect bites.

These are particularly important in the tropics. Conditions spread in this way include yellow fever, malaria and many others. It has been suggested that insect bites have contributed substantially to the rapid spread of AIDS in Central Africa although other authorities consider this unlikely. Theoretically, blood-borne viruses such as HIV and HBV could be spread by blood-sucking insects such as gnats. The risk of HIV spreading in this way is usually discounted in the UK.

THE BODY'S DEFENCES AGAINST INFECTION

The body possesses a wide range of defences against invading organisms. Many are extremely complex. Broadly they can be classified into two groups:

Innate (inborn or built-in) defences are those which are present regardless of any previous infection.

Acquired defences. When the body is infected by an organism it tends to develop defences specifically against that organism.

This is, of course, the principle of **prophylactic inoculation**. Here the body develops resistance against future infections after the injection of dead or **attenuated** bacteria or viruses. Attenuated organisms are those whose virulence has been reduced in some way whilst retaining antigenicity (for example, yellow fever vaccine – see page 20).

These mechanisms will now be examined in more detail.

INNATE DEFENCES

The most basic innate defences are mechanical barriers such as the skin. Skin-piercing procedures break this barrier.

Skin secretions kill some bacteria but are ineffective against others. The secretion of the stomach, being highly acid, destroys most organisms although *M. tuberculosis* is resistant. Commensals may occupy sites which otherwise might be colonised by invaders, thus limiting the threat.

Blood plasma (the liquid part of the blood) contains several substances which may destroy bacteria or facilitate their destruction by other mechanisms. One such substance is **complement** which facilitates **phagocytosis**.

Phagocytes are white blood cells which engulf invading organisms – a process known as phagocytosis. There are two main types of phagocytes, the **polymorphonuclear leucocytes**, or **polymorphs**, and the **macrophages**. Polymorphs resemble amoebae. They are motile and circulate freely in the blood stream. Macrophages are large cells with a single nucleus and they occur in two distinct situations. Some circulate in the blood stream like polymorphs. Others are attached to the linings of blood vessels and sinuses (cavities) in such organs as the liver, spleen, lymph-nodes and bone marrow. The macrophages collectively form what is known as the **reticulo-endothelial system**.

The above description applies to bacteria. The body's defence against viruses is much less clearly understood, although virus invasion is a frequent event. The reticulo-endothelial system may be involved as may certain smaller **lymphocytes** (see page 36). Interferon (see page 20), also seems to possess important anti-viral activity. Whatever the invader, the body's ability to defend itself may be modified by other factors such as age, nutrition and genetic factors.

ACQUIRED DEFENCES

There are two types of acquired immunity: antibody-mediated and cell-mediated.

Antibody-mediated immunity
Antigen/antibody reactions were discussed briefly on pages 8–9. Antibodies belong to a specialised class of proteins called **immunoglobulins** (abbreviated to Ig).

Lymphocytes are small nucleated white blood cells which originate in the bone-marrow. Two types are important here: B-lymphocytes and T-lymphocytes. B-lymphocytes are found mainly in **lymphoid tissue** which includes the lymph nodes, spleen, tonsils, etc. They produce immunoglobulins including antibodies.

Cell-mediated immunity

T-lymphocytes occur mainly in the circulating blood. There are several types including **T-helper cells** and **suppressor cells**. They respond to antigens to become involved in various aspects of immunity. These are known collectively as 'cell-mediated immunity'.

ANTIGENS AND ANTIBODIES

Bacteria and viruses contain specific antigens which stimulate the production of corresponding antibodies by the immune system.

The detection and identification of antibodies in the patient is an important means of deciding whether he is or has been infected by a particular organism. This general principle is widely used in diagnosis. In the case of virus infections it is often the only method available. A patient is said to be **seropositive** for a disease when appropriate antibodies can be detected in his blood. The term **seroconversion** is often used to indicate the time at which antibodies first become detectable.

This account of immunity is an over-simplification of a subject which involves many aspects of physiology and medicine, and which is developing rapidly. Any further discussion is beyond the scope of this book which cannot give more than the briefest insight into its complexity. Interested readers are referred to up-to-date books on medical microbiology for further information. (See Chapter 10.)

DISEASES WHICH MAY BE TRANSMITTED BY BEAUTY AND HEALTH-CARE WORKERS

The most serious infections which could be passed between clients by cross-infection are those which are carried in the blood.

Infected blood, tissue fluids or fragments may be transmitted between clients by skin-piercing procedures. Minute quantities of material can carry substantial amounts of infection and needles do not need to have visible contamination to be infective. It has been calculated that one millilitre of blood from an infective hepatitis B sufferer would be sufficient to infect more than 12 000 persons. Infection is not merely transmitted when the same unsterilised needle is used on successive patients although this is the most potent route of cross-infection. Where an operator handles infected equipment his hands become contaminated and so does everything else he touches. This will be discussed in more detail in Chapter 7.

At the time of writing, hepatitis B is the most important disease transmitted in this way. AIDS may well become a major problem in the near future. These conditions will be examined in detail.

HEPATITIS

Hepatitis – inflammation of the liver – can have many causes including infection by amoebae and viruses. Often, but not always, **jaundice** is associated with liver disease.

At the end of their useful life (normally about 120 days) red blood cells break down and part of their haemoglobin content is converted to a pigment called **bilirubin**. This is normally removed by the liver and excreted via the bile into the gut. It becomes the colouring matter of the faeces. Some is also modified and excreted in the urine. In liver disease this process may be upset so that bilirubin levels in the blood rise and cause a yellow colouration of the eyes, skin and certain body fluids. This increase in blood bilirubin and associated yellow staining is known as jaundice. There may also be a redistribution of colouring matter between the urine and the faeces, the former becoming very dark and the latter very light.

Hepatitis caused by viruses is the condition of most interest to readers of this book and hepatitis viruses are classified into one of three categories:
- Hepatitis A virus (HAV) causing **hepatitis type A**, also known as **infective hepatitis** or **short incubation hepatitis**.
- Hepatitis B virus (HBV) causing **hepatitis type B – serum**, or **long incubation hepatitis**.
- Non-A, non-B hepatitis viruses, causing hepatitis which cannot be categorised either A or B.

Hepatitis A virus is well understood and is a non-enveloped RNA virus.

It is present in the faeces of an infected person and normally spread by faecal contamination of food or water. It has an incubation period of about one month (20–40 days) and is very common in large closed communities living in primitive conditions. It is only very rarely transmitted parenterally and is therefore not of importance in skin-piercing. The symptoms are similar to those seen in hepatitis B although usually less severe and the death-rate is less than 0.1 per cent.

Liver disease and liver cancer in later life, not infrequent in hepatitis B cases are rarely seen following hepatitis A. Similarly, although carriers of hepatitis B are normally carriers for life, hepatitis A carriers tend to lose their carrier status quite quickly.

Hepatitis B virus (HBV) is an enveloped DNA virus. Much of our information about it has been derived from a study of its surface antigen, known as HBsAg (Hepatitis B Surface Antigen).

The virus is capable of surviving for long periods, possibly several years, on inert surfaces such as laboratory benches and this property gave it the reputation of being a sort of super-virus capable, perhaps, of resisting commonly used chemical disinfectants.

Because the virus cannot be grown on tissue culture, comparative testing of virucides (see page 45) on it have, until recently, not been carried out. Since most animals were immune, testing by this means was also not available. In a recent American paper, however, Bond et al.[1] reported treating a known virulent culture of HBV with various common disinfectants. These included 70 per cent isopropyl alcohol, Cidex, Sporicidin, sodium hypochlorite and an iodine containing compound (see Chapter 6). The culture was then injected into chimpanzees. None of these developed the disease and none displayed antibodies to it in serological testing.

A similar result, also using chimpanzees, has been reported from Japan by Kobayashi et al.[2] In this study, one sample of virus was heated for only two minutes at 98 °C. Other samples were treated with similar disinfectants to those used in Bond's work.

Due to their expense, only small numbers of chimpanzees were used and the results are not, therefore, statistically significant. Nevertheless, in all cases the treated culture failed to infect the test animals although several were subsequently infected by an untreated culture.

Therefore the indications are that normal sterilising and disinfectant procedures are likely to be effective against HBV. Equally, however, its long survival potential at room temperature emphasises the need for good **aseptic methods** (see Chapters 4 and 7) where clients may be at risk.

In the past it was thought that hepatitis B infection was entirely dependent on the transfer of infected blood from a carrier or sufferer to a recipient. It is now believed that transfer by other routes, not as yet clearly understood, is not uncommon.

The incubation period of the disease is 40 to 150 days – much longer than with hepatitis A. During most of the incubation period, patients are highly infectious.

The earliest symptoms are fever, accompanied by intense loss of appetite, often with nausea and vomiting. Jaundice may develop but this is not inevitable. Patients may feel severely ill for several months and a long convalescence is the rule. Most patients recover uneventfully but deaths do occur and rarely, in some outbreaks, mortality rates of 20 per cent have been reported. The main problem with the disease, however, is the long period of feeling unwell. In addition, patients probably have an increased risk of fatal liver cancer in later life.

Outbreaks associated with procedures such as tattooing, ear-piercing and acupuncture have been recorded. These involved cross-infection of 30 or more clients from one possible source. At least one death associated with tattooing is recorded.[3-6]

Symptomless carriers of the disease are common – 175 000 000 worldwide has been quoted – and highly infectious women carriers usually pass on the infection to their offspring at birth. The disease is very common amongst drug addicts sharing needles. Health-care workers and members of the beauty professions are at risk, especially from accidental needle-stabs.

Preventive inoculation against HBV is now available involving three injections of vaccine. All workers at risk should consider being inoculated to protect themselves from a very real environmental hazard. General practitioners should be able to provide advice and the necessary injections.

Hepatitis non-A non-B. It appears that at least two other distinct viruses apart from HAV and HBV are responsible for some outbreaks of hepatitis, both where the route is parenteral and where it is water-borne. The incubation period is usually 35–70 days and the clinical progress is similar to that of hepatitis B.

AIDS – ACQUIRED IMMUNE DEFICIENCY SYNDROME

This is an apparently new disease, the consequences of which were first noted amongst homosexual men in 1978–9.

It was first reported as a disease entity in the *New England Medical Journal* in 1981, and at the end of the same year the first case was reported in the UK. By mid-1986 465 cases had been reported in the UK, 77 per cent of whom were in the London area with most of the remainder in other large centres of population. By mid-1988 reported HIV positive cases in the UK had risen to 8794; 1598 of these had developed AIDS of whom 897 had died. Continuing escalation seems inevitable.

The organism is a retrovirus now known as HIV (Human Immunodeficiency Virus). It is not a particularly resistant virus and appears to be destroyed by normal disinfectant and sterilisation methods.[7]

Infection occurs primarily by the introduction of infected blood by a route other than the alimentary tract, or by heterosexual or homosexual contact. The early cases were almost all amongst homosexual men, especially those who had many different sexual partners. In the UK and other developed countries the most rapidly increasing group now is that of injecting drug-users who share syringes, and their sexual partners of either sex.

Thus, from being primarily a disease of males it is now increasingly being seen in women. Spread by normal heterosexual intercourse is therefore becoming more common. Parity between the sexes is already approaching in Africa and this seems likely to become the pattern elsewhere.

Haemophiliacs were another important group at risk. Haemophilia is a disease in which the blood-clotting mechanism is impaired. It occurs only in males but is carried genetically by females. Treatment involves giving a human blood derivative. The donor of this blood could have been infected by HIV. These derivatives are now heat-treated to eliminate the risk so further cases amongst haemophiliacs are unlikely.

The virus interferes with the immune system by attacking the **T-helper lymphocytes** thus impairing the body's resistance to disease. In this situation, known as **immunosuppression**, opportunistic infections develop against which the body has little defence.

Opportunistic infections are caused by organisms which are normally present in the body but are kept in check by the immune system. In the ordinary population the diseases they cause are very rare. In the absence of immunity such organisms take the opportunity to produce active infection. The common infections are pneumonia, particularly when caused by a protist called *Pneumocystis carinii*, and a skin cancer known as Kaposi's sarcoma, but these are not by any means the only opportunistic infections seen. Since the immunosuppression is ongoing, cure of one opportunistic infection, if a cure is available, still leaves the affected person liable to further attack from a different source.

There are several stages to the disease and not every infected person displays all stages.

A mild viral illness similar to glandular fever may develop some four to six weeks after infection. Later a more persistent enlargement of the lymph nodes may appear. Another possible development is ARC (AIDS-Related Complex) in which the patient has severe malaise, fatigue, diarrhoea and weight-loss. Some patients have developed brain disease resembling dementia. Finally, of course, AIDS may develop.

As the name implies, patients are only said to be suffering from AIDS when immunosuppression has taken place and they are therefore susceptible to fatal opportunistic infections. As more people who have had HIV infection for longer periods of time are recorded in the statistics, it appears that an increasing proportion will ultimately develop full-blown AIDS. A year or two ago this was considered likely to be about 30 per cent, but many authorities now believe that the figure could become 50 per cent or more.

As with most virus diseases, diagnosis depends on serological testing. Infected persons become seropositive (i.e. have detectable antibodies in their blood) at around two to three months after infection. This time is, however, very variable and may be anything from three weeks to a year or more. It is thought that all carriers of the virus, i.e. those who are serologically positive or will become so, are potentially infectious to others.

At the time of writing there is no proven treatment either for the immunosuppression or for the viral infection. Some of the opportunistic infections can be treated with antibiotics but the outlook for patients with developed AIDS is bleak. The antiviral drug zidovudine (formerly AZT) suppresses viral replication by interfering with the enzyme reverse transcriptase. This drug has substantial side effects. Others such as dideoxycytidine are under development and are claimed to have a reduced side effect risk. At present these drugs do little more than buy time for the patient.

The viral hepatitis B and HIV infections have now been discussed at length. Of the two, hepatitis B is currently the greatest problem for readers. It is more resistant and much more infectious than HIV and for the moment is much more common. It is, however, primarily a condition of inconvenience although it can be fatal, or lead to fatal after-effects. It is probably not seen as a problem by the general public.

HIV infection and AIDS are seen by the general public as serious diseases. Certainly for the patient who develops full-blown AIDS this is justified. Many patients are young and a fatal outcome is almost inevitable. Those who are infected by HIV and have not yet developed AIDS are dogged by fear of doing so.

The readers of this book will, in their work, have a great responsibility in avoiding cross-infecting their clients. These clients will rightly be worried about the risk, however small, of skin-piercing procedures and will need reassuring about hygiene and sterilisation methods in use. The remainder of this book is devoted to describing these methods and advising on the choice of the most appropriate ones.

REFERENCES

1. Bond et al., *Journal of Clinical Microbiology* 1983; 18; pp. 535-8.
2. Kobayashi et al., *Journal of Clinical Microbiology* 1984; 20; pp. 214-16.
3. Limentani et al., *Lancet* 1979; ii; pp. 86-8.
4. Harrison and Noah, *Lancet* 1980; ii; p. 644.
5. Hopkins et al., *British Medical Journal* 1973; ii; p. 210.
6. Boxall, *Journal of Medical Virology* 1978; 2; p. 377.
7. Spire et al., *Lancet* 1984; ii; pp. 899-901.

CHAPTER 4

Definitions

Many of the terms used in this book, such as sterilisation itself, conjure up a picture in the reader's mind, but it is necessary to understand *exactly* what they mean. In this short chapter the definitions of the various terms used in relation to sterilisation etc. are given.

It is important to have a clear picture of the precise meaning of these terms when considering suitable procedures to use in a practice. It is equally important in assessing the claims made for a new product or procedure before using it.

In the UK standard definitions are laid down in the British Standard Glossary of Terms relating to Disinfectants (BS 5283 of 1976). In the following sections these will be referred to as the BS definitions. In the USA slight variations exist and these are also summarised. Where the terms are used in other chapters of this book, they are used in the sense of the BS definition.

STERILISATION

This is an absolute term – there is no such condition as partial sterility. An object is either sterile or it isn't.

The BS definition is, 'the total removal or destruction of all living micro-organisms'. A few chemical disinfectants are capable of producing sterility under suitable conditions, but in general, sterility is produced by heat or irradiation methods.

Because it is difficult to prove a negative state, some workers have proposed as a definition that sterilisation is the process by which living organisms are removed or killed to the extent that they are no longer detectable in standard culture media in which they have previously been found to proliferate. To the purist, this is probably a more accurate definition.

DISINFECTANT

The BS definition is that this term is applied to a chemical agent which destroys micro-organisms but not usually bacterial spores.

It does not necessarily kill all micro-organisms but reduces them to a level which is neither harmful to health nor to the quality of perishable goods. The term is applicable to agents used to treat inanimate objects and materials and may also be applied to agents used to treat the skin and other body membranes and cavities.

In the USA, the concept of using the word in relation to application to the human body is frowned upon. The word tends to be used for substances intended to be applied to inanimate objects only.

It is interesting to note that in the seventeenth century, when the word 'disinfect' was first used, disease tended to be associated with unpleasant smells. To be effective, disinfectants were expected to remove these odours or at least to mask them. To many people this concept of odour-elimination still prevails. A popular disinfectant will sell much better if it has the right kind of 'fresh' odour.

Readers should be careful not to assess products on subjective characteristics such as odour. Clearly if a disinfectant is doing its job, it will prevent the development of odours following bacterial breakdown of protein, etc. Once such breakdown has occurred odours will not necessarily be removed even if the organisms have been killed.

ANTISEPTIC

This word means 'against putrefaction' and antiseptics were originally used to prevent the decay of meat and other organic materials. The word is defined by the BS as 'a chemical agent which destroys or inhibits micro-organisms on living tissues, having the effect of limiting or preventing the harmful results of infection'.

Traditionally, the image of an antiseptic has veered towards inhibition of growth rather than towards destruction – to be bacteriostatic rather than bactericidal. The legal definition in the USA, however, requires an antiseptic to be germicidal unless it is, by nature, something such as an ointment which is intended to be in prolonged contact with the body.

Definitions of the words 'disinfectant' and 'antiseptic' and the concepts which they represent, have varied substantially over the years. One authority mentions studying 143 definitions of 'disinfectant' and 165 of 'antiseptic' made over the 100 years or so prior to 1930.

BACTERICIDE

The BS definition is, 'a chemical agent which, under defined conditions, is capable of killing bacteria but not necessarily bacterial spores'.

The term is applied to all bacteria, pathogenic or non-pathogenic, but not necessarily to other micro-organisms such as fungi etc. The word is more commonly used as the adjective – bactericidal.

A **germicide** is a chemical agent which destroys micro-organisms including fungi, viruses, etc., but not necessarily spores. It is thus virtually identical to 'disinfectant' and again is more commonly used in its adjectival form.

It is worth noting that if a product is claimed solely to be bactericidal it may not destroy viruses. Its value could therefore be limited if viruses such as HBV or HIV were present.

BACTERIOSTAT

This is defined by BS as, 'a chemical agent which, in defined conditions, is capable of inhibiting the multiplication of a bacterial population'.

The terms **fungistat** and **biostat** are also used, especially in American literature, referring to the inhibition of growth of fungi and of all living things.

VIRUCIDE, SPORICIDE, FUNGICIDE AND BIOCIDE

These are words implying the destruction of: a) viruses, b) spores, c) fungi, d) all forms of life.

A biocide, since it kills everything including spores, presumably implies a sterilising agent.

ASEPTIC METHODS

As will be seen, thorough cleaning alone will remove most bacteria etc. from surfaces.

When care is taken to avoid infection by clean and orderly working habits rather than by allowing infection to appear and then applying disinfectants etc., it is said that **aseptic methods** have been used. Thus, these are working methods which are aimed at avoiding infection rather than attacking it.

ANTIBIOTIC

It is useful to know the definition of this term, although it is not used in this book.

A recent American book defines it as, 'an organic chemical substance, produced by micro-organisms, which in dilute solution can destroy or inhibit the growth of bacteria or other micro-organisms. It is used, usually in low concentration, in the treatment of infectious diseases of man, animals or plants'.

CHAPTER 5
Sterilisation

The theoretical background of sterilisation and the monitoring of its effectiveness are discussed in this chapter.

Preliminary cleaning is described, followed by consideration of the various methods of sterilising available. These are then assessed for use on the small scale which applies to most readers of this book. Lastly the types of equipment that are available and suited to this market are mentioned.

As noted in the previous chapter, the term 'sterilisation' is absolute, implying the killing of all living organisms.

In advertisements, such terms as 'cold sterilising solution' may be used to describe certain preparations. Some of these, if used strictly in accordance with the maker's recommendation may, in fact, achieve sterility. The variables however, are such that it is customary not to accept any of these substances as sterilising agents. They are, nevertheless, efficient disinfectants and will be discussed in Chapter 6. They should only be used when the methods of sterilisation described here cannot reasonably be employed.

Before considering in detail the methods of sterilisation available, some background to the subject is required. When exposed to a sterilisation process, not every organism is killed at once, or at the same time. Despite the definition of sterilisation there will always be a slight risk of occasional failure and we need to look at the implications of this.

Some procedures result in very rapid death of the organisms, whilst others are slower. Exposure to steam at 134 °C produces sterility much more quickly than exposure at 121 °C. Methods which kill rapidly are less likely to leave any live organisms than those which are slower. Similarly, if a large number of organisms is present before sterilisation, there is a greater risk that they will not all be killed. This is one important reason for ensuring that articles to be sterilised are cleaned beforehand, removing gross contamination.

To put figures on the risk, a process is unacceptable if, for every 100 articles 'sterilised', one still contains a viable organism. However, the risk is probably acceptable if only one article in 1 000 000 remains incompletely sterile.

TESTS FOR EFFICIENCY OF STERILISATION

On a commercial or hospital scale, regular monitoring of the performance of sterilisers is a routine procedure. Where heat is the sterilising medium, temperature gauges or thermocouples are built into the equipment. Pressure gauges are included in steam equipment although, as will be seen, steam pressure alone does not produce sterility.

In their work, readers will not be sterilising wrapped articles or textile materials such as dressings so the sterilising medium, steam or hot air, has direct and unrestricted access to the infected surfaces. There is then little likelihood of incomplete exposure.

Under commercial or hospital conditions, articles such as wrapped dressings, large bottles of liquid, bundles of towels, bedding, etc. need sterilising. The penetration of heat into the innermost recesses of dressings packs can be a problem. Tightness of bundling, size of bundles, etc. are important.

In these circumstances, some form of indicator included within the bundle may be used to show that sterilising conditions have been attained. For this purpose, coloured paper strips or tapes (Bowie–Dick Test) or tubes of a suitable liquid (Browne's tubes) are used. These contain chemicals which change colour when sterilising conditions have been attained.

Browne's TST strips[1] for steam autoclaves are paper strips bearing a yellow patch which changes to purple when sterilising conditions of time, steam and temperature have been attained. Several different versions are available covering all the commonly used time/temperature combinations. The colour change is rapid and unequivocal and takes place only after all the conditions have been satisfied[2]. These strips are very inexpensive and it is recommended that they are always used in small scale autoclaves (see page 59) as a check on performance.

Similar colour-change markers are included in commercial gamma-irradiated products (see page 51) where a change from yellow to red indicates that irradiation has occurred. Markers are also available for ethylene oxide sterilisation monitoring (see page 52).

The ultimate test is, of course, bacteriological examination of the articles undergoing sterilisation. Test packs of suitable non-pathogenic organisms such as the spores of *B. subtilis* are often included in the load. At the end of the process this material is incubated in culture media which are then examined for bacterial growth. This kind of monitoring involves equipment which would not normally be available to readers of this book. It is, however, used widely on a hospital or commercial scale.

Most of the equipment likely to be used by the reader will have temperature and/or pressure gauges, or be manufactured in such a manner as to give predictable results. Performance will have been checked exhaustively in the design and prototype stages. To monitor performance in use by including a TST strip or similar in every autoclave load is a sensible and inexpensive check.

CLEANING OF ARTICLES BEFORE STERILISATION

Whatever method of sterilisation or disinfection is being used, contaminated articles must be physically clean. There are several reasons for this:
- To remove any residual organic material from the previous patient, bearing in mind that contamination need not be visible to carry a very real threat of infection.
- The cleaning process reduces the amount of infective material remaining which improves the likelihood of the sterilisation process being complete.
- Grease and oily material may prevent the penetration of steam or aqueous disinfectant to any infected surface which it covers.
- Instruments not cleaned before the application of heat may in time become covered with a hard impenetrable film of partly charred organic material. This not merely interferes with sterilisation but results in progressive deterioration of the instrument. It is particularly likely to happen when dry heat is used.

Manual cleaning, before sterilisation, by soaking in a cold detergent such as a solution of washing-up liquid, followed by careful scrubbing with a stiff brush and rinsing under running water should be adequate for small instruments.

Ordinary soaps, unlike synthetic detergents produce insoluble scums with hard water which interfere with the cleaning process and should not be used.

Particular care should be paid to inaccessible parts of instruments such as the area of forceps between the blades where they meet to form the handle. Such equipment should be bought with a view to ease of cleaning. Forceps are available that are easy to clean between the blades, right up to the point where they meet.

Operators must be very careful not to inflict small cuts or stabs on themselves whilst handling unsterilised 'sharps'. (This term is used to describe any sharp instrument.) (See also Chapter 7.)

Ultrasonic cleaning

Specialised equipment in which ultrasonic vibrations in a liquid are used to induce cleaning are available. The vibrations loosen and detach material adhering to instruments, especially in nooks and crannies, more successfully than scrubbing. This is recommended for tattooists in cleaning their equipment before sterilisation. It can also be used with advantage by other operators.

STERILISATION METHODS AVAILABLE

The following general methods of sterilisation are available:
- Radiation
- Gases
- Heat – dry heat or moist heat

With minor exceptions the first two of these are not suitable for small scale use. They may however, have been employed on equipment bought ready sterilised. They will be mentioned briefly. The methods which readers are likely to use will then be discussed in more detail.

RADIATION

Two types of radiation are used in sterilising, **ionising** and **non-ionising**. For ionising radiation **gamma rays** or **high energy electrons** are used. **Ultraviolet light** is the source of non-ionising radiation.

Gamma irradiation, using a radioisotope source such as cobalt-60, is used extensively on a commercial scale. Readers are likely to use products such as needles which have been sterilised in this way. The method is widely used for disposable products. The packages normally contain a colour-change indicator showing that sterilising conditions have been attained.

This sterilising method is highly efficient and since there is only a negligible temperature rise it can be used on heat-sensitive materials. Nevertheless the radiation itself can cause deterioration of some plastics or rubber, especially if repeated, but apart from this it is an excellent method.

It has the further advantage that articles to be sterilised can be prepacked. Further packaging and handling in the factory therefore need not be done under sterile conditions. Gamma irradiation is totally unsuitable for small-scale use.

Ultraviolet radiation (UVR) of a suitable wavelength has been in use for many years as a germicide.

In the past this was a popular method of 'sterilising' in beauty and hairdressing salons and UV cabinets are still seen in some establishments. For several reasons this is no longer considered an appropriate method.

It is only effective against a limited range of organisms. Vegetative bacteria are the most susceptible and fungal spores are highly resistant.

Penetration is extremely limited. Only small numbers of susceptible organisms on an otherwise clean and exposed surface are killed. Clumps of organisms and even dust on surfaces may protect organisms from penetration.

The output of UV lamps decreases with time.

Ultraviolet radiation should no longer be regarded as a sterilising agent and the use of UV cabinets for this purpose should be discontinued.

Its main use is in controlling airborne organisms to maintain conditions in aseptic rooms or work-areas.

GASES

The gases **ethylene oxide** and **formaldehyde** are used as sterilising agents. They act by combining into the chemical structure of proteins in the organism.

Some increase in temperature is desirable to speed up the process. With ethylene oxide a range of 20-56 °C is used and with formaldehyde up to 70 °C. The relative humidity in the sterilising chamber is accurately controlled – since low levels may result in incomplete sterilisation. The optimum level varies with the different gases. The actual amount of gas present is also important. Pre-wrapping is not possible since it prevents penetration of the gas.

Ethylene oxide is generally preferred but has the disadvantage of forming explosive mixtures with air.

Materials sterilised by gases need thorough aeration before use. On a commercial scale the articles are 'washed through' with filtered air after treatment to remove residual gas. The method is used on a large scale for articles such as blankets and other textiles but for most industrial applications gamma irradiation is preferred.

Small-scale apparatus which could be suitable for clinic use is marketed in some countries including the USA. It comprises a closed vessel with small chambers for water and propylene oxide, heated under thermostatic control. Propylene oxide is chemically closely related to ethylene oxide. Being liquid at room temperature it is easier to handle on a small scale.

For small metal instruments such as those used by readers of this book, autoclaving is simpler and more reliable. (See pages 57-65.)

HEAT

Sterilisation by heat, especially on a small or medium scale, is the most effective and economical method. Its main disadvantage is that many articles cannot, without deterioration, be heated to the temperatures required.

Either dry heat or moist heat may be used. The presence of water in suitably controlled conditions results in sterilisation at substantially lower temperatures than when dry heat is used. On the other hand, the apparatus required for moist-heat sterilisation is usually more complex and more expensive than that for dry heat. Before considering both methods in detail the basic principles will be examined.

Times and temperatures

With all heat sterilising devices, whether for moist or dry heat, it is the combination of temperature and time of exposure which ensures sterility. When discussing moist heat the importance of pressure will also be mentioned.

Pressure alone does not sterilise. It is only important in raising the boiling point of water and, on a commercial scale, in ensuring steam penetration of packages of textiles.

For the actual process of sterilisation **holding time** is the important factor. This is the time required to sterilise the load at the selected operating temperature.

Holding time varies with the organism and is substantially longer for spores than for vegetative forms of bacteria. The time required to kill a particular organism at a given temperature is the **thermal death time** (TDT). The holding time is often taken as the thermal death time for a temperature 10 °C below that being used for sterilisation. Thus if the TDT of an organism is 30 minutes at 150 °C a suitable holding time for sterilising at 160 °C would be 30 minutes. This allows for temperature variations within the chamber of the steriliser.

Other important times are:

a) **heating-up time** – the time taken for the steriliser to attain sterilising temperature.

b) **heat penetration time** – the time taken after the load is inserted in the steriliser for all parts of it to reach sterilising temperature, and for the whole to re-stabilise at that temperature.

c) **safety time** – a safety time addition of 50 per cent is usually added to the holding time.

Thus **sterilising time** becomes:

Heat penetration time + Holding time + Safety time.

On a small scale, arbitrary times which take all the above into account, are usually recommended by equipment makers. These times are built into the operating cycle of small machines such as automatic autoclaves. They also take account of the type of load for which the machine is intended.

Dry heat

Dry heat below 140 °C does not destroy bacterial spores in an acceptable time so normally temperatures in the range 150-80 °C are used. Indeed some more sophisticated apparatus works at 280 °C on a relatively short time cycle.

The usual apparatus, suitable for small scale use, is the **hot air oven**. Small models such as that illustrated here are electrically heated with a fan to assist air circulation. There is protection against overheating and a dial thermometer is fitted. The model illustrated has a chamber size 29 × 19 × 18 cm.

The Medical Research Council (MRC) has issued recommended exposure times (i.e. holding time plus safety time) for hot air ovens of:

Temperature (°C)	Exposure time, min.
160	45
170	18
180	$7\frac{1}{2}$
190	$1\frac{1}{2}$

SES Mistral hot air oven showing temperature selector, thermometer and timer, with monitoring lights and perforated instrument trays.

A second dry heat method suitable for very small articles is the **glass bead steriliser**.

Typical models are illustrated on page 56. They consist of an electrically heated box surrounded by a protective insulated case or cover, and containing one or more small cylindrical chambers. These are filled with minute glass spheres or beads. Needles for sterilisation are inserted as deeply as possible into the beads which transfer heat to them in a similar manner to immersion in a liquid. A disadvantage is that the needle cannot be immersed fully so the projecting part may remain unsterilised.

Working temperatures range between 190-300 °C, varying from one model to another, with sterilising times ranging from 1-10 minutes. Heating up times vary from about 20-50 minutes, again depending on model.

For the limited purpose for which they are intended, and provided that the needles are not damaged by the temperatures attained, these inexpensive devices will sterilise. They are, of course, quite unsuitable for all but the smallest articles.

Potential users should bear in mind the limitations of glass bead sterilisers. Since they are in no sense automatic, close adherence to the maker's instructions is essential. In particular, care must be taken that the full heating up time is allowed and that immersion for the full recommended holding and safety times are followed. These times vary from one model to another and it is most important to understand and follow the instructions.

The market for dry heat equipment is expected to diminish substantially as automatic autoclaves become cheaper.

Before leaving dry heat sterilisation, a brief mention should be made of **flaming** and **incineration**.

These methods involve destruction by fire. In laboratory work the outsides of test-tubes and their cotton wool plugs are passed through a flame before opening. The platinum loops used for inoculating media before culture are heated to redness after use.

Incineration is the destruction of an article by burning and is recommended for the disposal of used dressings etc. This will be discussed further in Chapter 7.

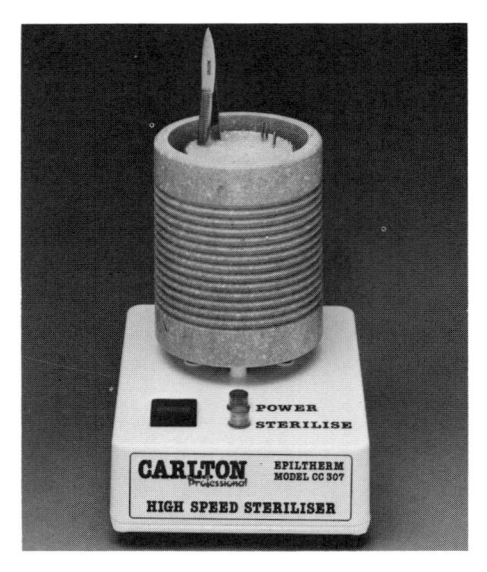

Carlton Professional Epiltherm glass bead steriliser. The controls can be seen in the base, whilst the circular tower is an insulating casing surrounding the central cavity in which the beads are heated. Forceps and electrolysis needles are shown partly immersed in the beads.

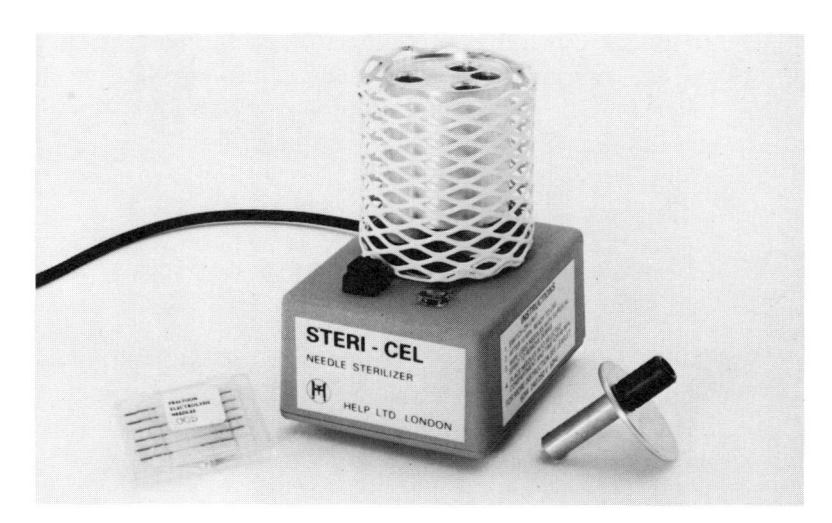

Steri-Cel glass bead steriliser by HELP Ltd of London. The expanded metal heat shield surrounding the bead-chamber protects the operator. The small circular chambers seen in the top contains the beads and a lid is provided, (right). Again, the controls are seen in the base.

Moist heat

Moist heat kills by coagulation of bacterial protoplasm – like the setting of egg-white when boiled.

Although most vegetative forms of bacteria are killed by boiling in water for five minutes, bacterial spores are not destroyed and some viruses may also be resistant. The process of boiling in water is therefore at best a disinfectant procedure only.

In older surgical catalogues, attractive looking chromium-plated electrically heated boxes were often illustrated. In these, trays of small instruments were boiled in water. These devices were frequently described as 'instrument sterilisers' although obviously they do not sterilise. They are now, more accurately, called instrument boilers.

For moist heat sterilisation, it is essential to attain temperatures of 110–35 °C and the usual range is 121–34 °C.

Water boils under atmospheric pressure at 100 °C, but if the pressure over the boiling water is increased, the temperature at which the water boils is raised. Thus, if water is heated in a closed vessel, constructed to withstand the higher pressures attained, the water/steam temperatures achieved readily reach the 110–35 °C range needed for sterilisation.

A pressure vessel like this is known as an **autoclave**. Strictly, the word 'autoclave' means a vessel whose lid is automatically sealed under pressure but the term has now come to mean a vessel for sterilising by steam at temperatures above 100 °C under pressure.

Steam is a valuable agent for sterilising for several reasons. Chief amongst these are its low cost and its high **latent heat of vapourisation**.

A considerable amount of heat is needed to change water from its liquid state at boiling point to its gaseous state, steam, at the same temperature. This is known as the latent heat of vapourisation. When steam is condensed to water, this heat is given up again so that articles heated by steam rapidly attain working temperature.

Two factors are important in moist-heat sterilisation: the steam must be at the right temperature and it must be saturated.

Saturated steam is such that when it is cooled only very slightly, water will start to condense out. It may be heated to higher temperatures and this is often done in boilers producing steam for power. Steam which is much hotter than its saturation point is said to be superheated and is no more efficient for sterilising than any other hot gas.

To establish the pressure/temperature relationships shown in the next paragraph, air must be eliminated from the autoclave. This is particularly important since otherwise the temperatures reached will be lower than the pressure suggests and sterilisation may not be achieved. All autoclaves for sterilising incorporate some means of removing the air trapped inside.

The following table shows the effect of increased pressure on the boiling point of water:

Pressure (p.s.i. or lb/in^2)	Boiling point (°C)
10	115
15	121
20	126
32	134

For sterilising by moist heat, the MRC recommendations are:

    3 minutes at 134 °C.
    10 minutes at 126 °C.
    15 minutes at 121 °C.

As before, these are exposure times and contain both holding time and safety time factors. Additional penetration time is required but for small articles this will be very short.

Sterilisation by autoclave In large commercial autoclaves, as used in hospital sterilisation departments, the sterilising chamber is a large steel cylinder or box surrounded by a jacket which can be heated by admitting steam.

The autoclave is loaded with articles to be sterilised, the doors locked, and air evacuated by a pump. Steam at suitable pressure is then admitted to the chamber. The process of evacuation and steam admission may be repeated. When sterilisation time is complete, the contents are dried by again evacuating the chamber whilst also applying heat by admitting steam to the jacket. Apart from sterilising instruments this cycle of events is particularly suitable for dressings, towels, bedding, etc., which are delivered dry.

In small automatic instrument autoclaves such as readers may use there is no steam-heated jacket since the post-sterilisation drying facility is not required.

For this reason, the equipment is not suitable for sterilising textiles. There is no vacuum pump, heavy cold air being displaced from the bottom of the chamber by the relatively light hot steam which fills the chamber from the top. This process is known as **downward displacement**.

In the more sophisticated types, (see page 60) water is boiled by an electric element in the bottom of the chamber or in a separate small boiler. The steam produced rises to the top and drives out the air through a vent tube near the bottom of the chamber. The tube leads to a pressure loaded safety valve to exhaust into the atmosphere.

When the autoclave is loaded and the door closed, pressing the start button starts the cycle which is fully automatic.

The boiler fills with water from a reservoir, heats up, air is expelled and a system of indicator lights monitors the progress of the operation and its completion. Pressure gauges and thermometers and various safety devices are fitted. Some models give a single cycle only – 3 to $3\frac{1}{2}$ minutes at 134 °C – whilst others give a choice of time/temperature ranges. Complete cycle times at 134 °C are about 12 minutes. Little attention is normally required apart from keeping the reservoir topped up with deionised water.

Deionised water is usually used in this type of equipment. It is water from which all metallic salts, such as those which are found in hard water, have been removed. If hard water is used, deposits of these salts, precipitated by heating the water, collect as scale in the steriliser, interfering with heat-transfer, blocking tubes, etc. In some areas where soft water is available, this may be used.

A more simple type of automatic autoclave is now being marketed[3]. As it is moderately priced it should be ideal for general practitioners, beauty therapists, electrolysists, acupuncturists, hairdressers, chiropodists and health care workers of all types.

It has an adequate capacity for equipment such as racks, dishes, forceps, razors, needles etc. Various internal equipment is available, which can be adapted to the requirements of the above. Alternative equipment specifically designed for dental surgeons is also produced.

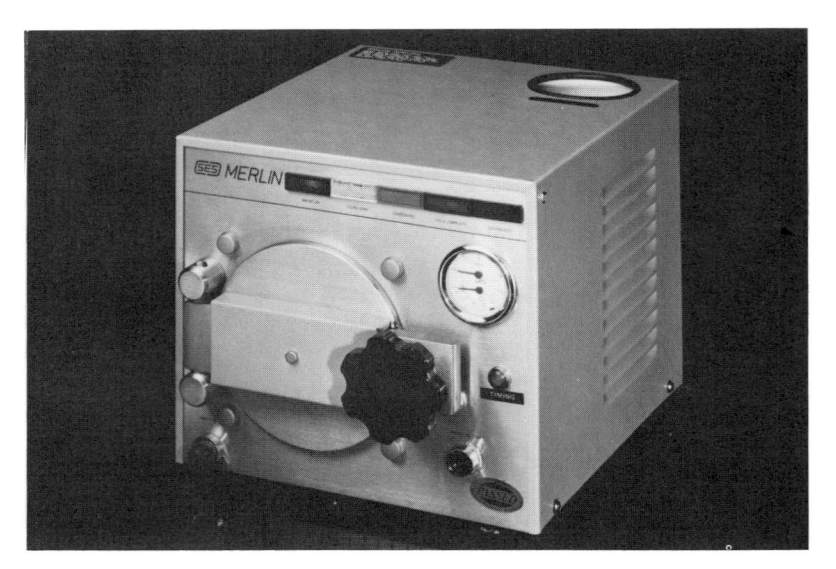

SES Merlin automatic autoclave. The large black knob is the locking device for the heavy circular stainless steel chamber door to its left. The monitoring lights and pressure gauge/thermometer dial can readily be seen. The boiler is filled through the circular opening on the top.

SES Little Sister 2 automatic autoclave. This is somewhat larger than the Merlin illustrated above. The chamber door is enclosed behind the cream-coloured door on the left front. The control panel on the right includes a pressure gauge and digital temperature readout.

A suitable volume of water (750 ml) is placed in the container, the items for sterilising are installed and the steriliser switched on. The cycle is then automatically controlled and monitored by indicator lights.

The machine operates on a 20 p.s.i./126 °C cycle for 11 minutes, the complete cycle taking about 35 minutes. This can be reduced to about 23 minutes using manual depressurisation at the end of the sterilising cycle. With its relatively large capacity it could probably be loaded at the end of the working day, switched on and left to run so that in the morning sterile equipment is ready for the day's work.

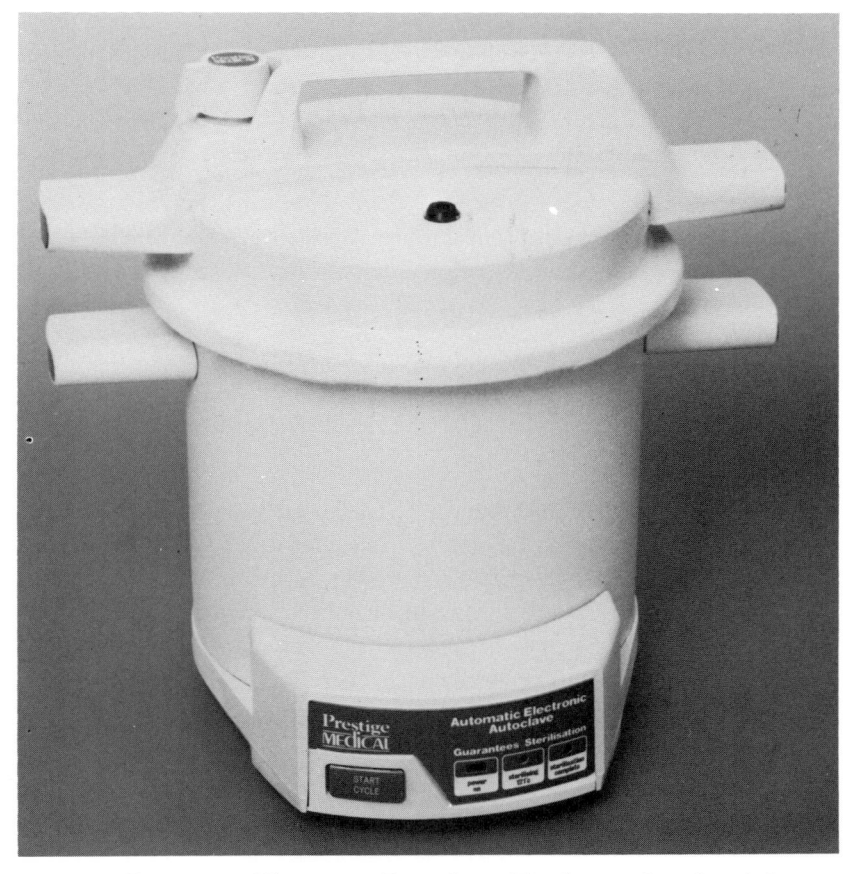

Prestige Automatic Electronic Autoclave. The large chamber lid is removed by turning partly anti-clockwise and lifting off. The simple controls, including a 'start cycle' button and monitor lights can be seen in the base.

The small autoclaves described above are all of the automatic type. No manual control is required once the machine has started its cycle. Temperature and time are attained without human intervention. As cheaper machines become available, operators will appreciate the convenience and ease of operation of a reliable automatic machine.

Because the human factor is eliminated, some authorities believe that only an automatic autoclave is suitable for use by non-technical personnel.

On the other hand, provided that an operator understands the importance of ensuring that the parameters of time and temperature are always attained, there is no reason why a basic appliance such as a **pressure cooker** should not be used. This has the particular advantage that the cooker is very simple with virtually nothing mechanical to go wrong. The motivation, responsibility and training of the operator should ensure its success.

According to Rubbo and Gardner[4] domestic pressure cookers offer a cheap and simple means of sterilising small articles by steam under pressure. Thermocouple measurements show that it is not difficult to expel air from so small a vessel.

An adaptation of one British pressure cooker is used world-wide as an autoclave in underdeveloped countries for sterilising injection equipment under a World Health Organization immunisation programme.

For pressure cookers a TST strip for the range 121 °C/15 minutes should *always* be used. It is preferable to use one frequently, if not always, in automatic autoclaves to monitor their operation. When a TST strip is used in an automatic autoclave it monitors the functioning of the machine. When used in a pressure cooker it also monitors the operator. It is because the operator could be a variable factor that it is particularly important to monitor him.

Pressure cookers are, in effect, small autoclaves. Water is placed in the cooker chamber and they are normally heated on a separate heat source such as an electric hotplate or gas ring.

For sterilising, about one litre of water is used (substantially more than for cooking because a large amount is lost as steam from the safety valve). The articles to be sterilised are placed on the trays in the cooker and initially a high rate of heating is applied. When the water boils and pressure is attained, steam emerges briskly from the safety valve. The steam expels the air from the cooker, and to achieve this the high rate of boiling is continued for five minutes.

The heat input is then reduced and timing of the sterilising cycle starts. During this part of the cycle steam must continue to emerge freely from the safety valve. This indicates that pressure is being maintained, since the safety valve is set to operate at 15 p.s.i. A

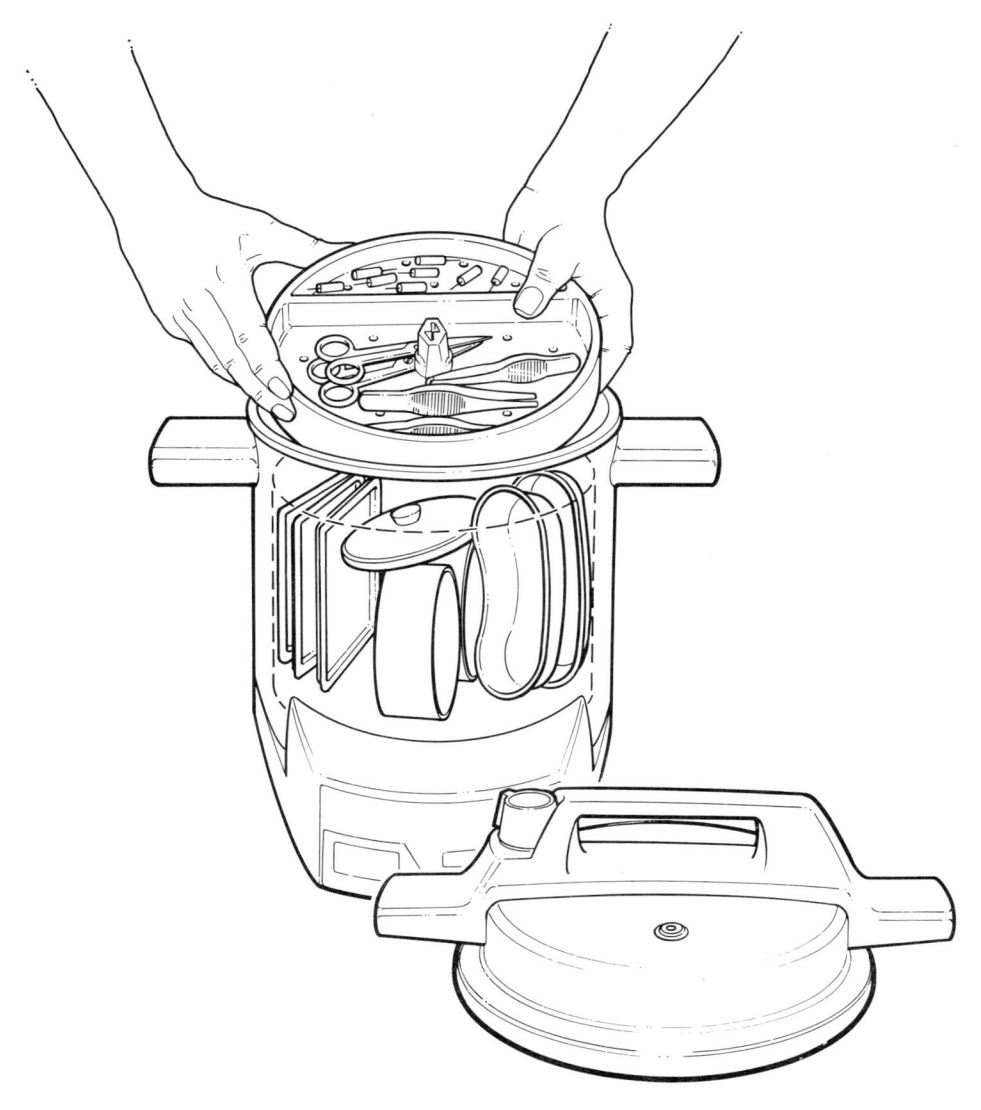

Loading an automatic autoclave.

sterilising time of 15 to 20 minutes is usually allowed. Before buying a pressure cooker the makers should be asked to confirm that the safety valve setting is 15 p.s.i. or more.

Care must be taken when loading autoclaves. With small autoclaves and pressure cookers, indeed with any machine not fitted with a vacuum pump, it is important that steam can enter all articles to be sterilised, and displace the air from them.

Hollow vessels such as small dishes should be placed on their sides and not inverted. Lids should be put in separately. If this is not done, large bubbles of air can be trapped in these dishes. If this happens the pressure/temperature relationships are upset and the saturated steam is not able to contact the surfaces where the bubbles are trapped.

Future developments in autoclave design and use. In most of the UK in the late 1980s legislation or codes of practice exist requiring that many articles used in hairdressing, various beauty procedures, electrolysis, tattooing, etc. be sterilised (see Chapter 9). The actual method of sterilising is not laid down. Enforcement of the law is in the hands of the Environmental Health Departments of local authorities, and officers of these departments need to rely on ill-defined sources for information on suitable sterilisation methods.

It is almost certain that autoclaving will become the method of choice but, in turn, standards for autoclaves have not yet evolved although the temperature/pressure/time relationships described earlier in this chapter are well accepted.

It is likely that there will be controversy about the monitoring of the performance of small automatic autoclaves. Whilst these machines are controlled electronically throughout their cycle and such control is normally very reliable, some form of independent monitoring that sterilising conditions have been attained in every cycle is essential. It is also desirable, if possible, that a record is kept to prove that this has been done. In large commercial autoclaves, eyeball checks on temperature gauges, pressure gauges and clocks are maintained by trained personnel and recorded graphically on charts by the gauges concerned. Internal indicators such as Browne's tubes, TST strips, etc. are also used.

The more expensive and sophisticated small automatic autoclaves are fitted with pressure and temperature gauges and these must be observed by operators during every cycle in accordance with the maker's instructions. There is no automatic recording of the information, however, unless a TST strip is also included.

Pressure and temperature gauges are relatively expensive items and the newer, cheaper autoclaves do not have them, although it is likely that versions of these machines fitted with gauges will become available at enhanced prices, for operators who prefer them. Such small machines rely on TST strips for monitoring.

It is in establishing the need for pressure/temperature gauge monitoring or otherwise that controversy is likely to develop. The author's personal belief is that, provided the accuracy and reliability of TST strips continues to be confirmed, these are probably adequate for monitoring cycle sterility achievement and that gauges are superfluous. This is because, if non-recording gauges are used (and no-one would contemplate using recording ones in small autoclaves) they need to be monitored constantly otherwise the monitoring is almost valueless. Assuming that the machine is reliable, the gauges will almost always give the same reading and, in a situation where sterilising is an operation secondary to the main functioning of the establishment, apathy in taking readings is inevitable, although it must be guarded against. The TST strip, however, gives a clear and unequivocal indication of condition attainment and can be dated and retained as evidence of this. In these circumstances, the expense of fitting gauges seems hardly justified.

No doubt standards for small automatic autoclaves will be established in the UK and in other developed countries. In the UK this will probably be in the form of a British Standard Specification (BSS). Intending purchasers of autoclaves should confirm with any controlling authority that the autoclaves they intend to buy comply with the regulations in force for the area in which they work.

SUMMARY

The lesson which should emerge from this chapter is that, for the small-scale worker, heat is the simplest and most effective sterilising agent. Moist heat is less damaging to equipment than dry heat and is generally preferable.

The important factors of timing and temperature cannot be over-stressed and it is the responsibility of the operator to ensure that these requirements are always fulfilled. To be successful, the operation of all automatic equipment must be monitored and it must be regularly serviced in the recommended way.

Finally, atmospheric pressure boilers, and chemical disinfectants, however advertised, are *not* sterilising agents. The methods described in this chapter are the only ones which, if used properly, will ensure sterility.

REFERENCES

1. TST strips are available from Albert Browne Ltd., Chancery House, Abbey Gate, Leicester, LE4 0AA, UK
2. R. Hambleton, *Sterile World*, April 1983.
3. Marketed by Prestige Medical, Prestige House, 14–18 Holborn, London, EC1N 2LQ, UK
4. Rubbo and Gardner, *A Review of Sterilisation and Disinfection*, published by Lloyd, Luke Ltd., London

CHAPTER 6

Disinfectants and antiseptics

It would be helpful to study products in these two groups separately. However, many substances are used for both purposes so it becomes more logical to look at the products and consider the purposes for which each can be used.

As in earlier chapters, the general background will be examined. The products available will then be listed and those of particular value in the beauty and health care fields will be considered in detail.

The market for the products discussed in this chapter is a large and valuable one and manufacturers compete keenly for their market share. Whilst no advertisement or representative would deliberately mislead, any information given should be examined critically before changing from an established product to a new one.

Products promoted to the professions as opposed to those promoted for household use are usually supported by third party evidence (TPE). Look especially for references to published work in reputable journals such as the *British Medical Journal, British Dental Journal, Lancet* or the *Pharmaceutical Journal*. When new preparations are introduced it is customary for their properties to be assessed by independant persons such as doctors or pharmacists. Their findings are then published in the journals and give support to manufacturers' claims. If in doubt ask a local pharmacist who will be glad to offer sound advice.

Don't be influenced in choice of product by subjective properties like odour. Household-type products advertised on television with a 'nice clean pine-smell' are unlikely to be much more than just that. This is not to say that premises should not smell nice – it is just that odour in this type of product is no measure of effectiveness.

The last general point is that humans have much in common with bacteria – both are constructed from basically similar materials. Anything which kills bacteria or viruses may well have unpleasant effects on persons handling it.

If substances which kill bacteria could be chosen without thought for other effects, the choice would be very wide. The substances used are highly active chemicals and must be handled with great care. The operator's and clients' exposure to them must be limited and they must generally be treated with due respect. The need for extra care will be mentioned where necessary with particular products but do remember always the overall need for caution.

DISINFECTION AND STERILISATION

Although it may be desirable to eliminate bacteria and viruses from the working environment, in practice this is impossible. The precautions taken depend both on the risk of the particular work and the practicality of reducing those risks. These aspects will be examined more closely in the next chapter but inevitably the result will be a compromise.

The greatest cross-infection risk occurs when there is piercing or cutting of the skin and for the needles etc., used nothing less than absolute sterility is acceptable. There *must* be a newly sterilised needle for every patient. Other equipment may also become contaminated and, if so, will need sterilising.

Where, because of the material used an article cannot be sterilised, it must be disinfected. Where disinfection is chosen rather than sterilisation, for what may be termed second-level-risk equipment, this choice may *only* be made on the grounds that sterilisation is physically impossible. That sterilisers are not available is not an excuse for accepting disinfection as an alternative. If sterilisation is needed and practicable it must be used.

FACTORS AFFECTING CHEMICAL DISINFECTANTS AND ANTISEPTICS

a) **Types of organisms**. By definition, most chemical disinfectants do not kill spores in a reasonable time. **Glutaraldehyde** is a notable exception and a few other substances have limited sporicidal activity. Most vegetative bacteria with the exception of the acid-fast ones are killed rapidly by most disinfectants. The killing of viruses is less certain although again glutaraldehyde and the **halogens** are effective.

b) Numbers of organisms. It was stated in Chapter 3 that before sterilisation or disinfection, articles must be thoroughly cleaned. Indeed at the level of disinfection, some authorities claim that disinfectants are not really necessary – a good scrubbing brush is all that is required. Certainly disinfection can never replace cleanliness.

c) Moisture. Normally, moisture must be present for disinfectants to be effective. Pure alcohol, for example, has little disinfectant effect on dry test organisms compared with 70 per cent alcohol – a mixture of 70 per cent alcohol with 30 per cent water.

d) Concentration. The concentrations of solutions of disinfectants and antiseptics recommended are normally a compromise between maximum effectiveness and minimum damage to operators and equipment.

Although water must be present, particular care must be taken not to 'dilute out' disinfectants. If more water is allowed to enter solutions in small quantities their concentration may be gradually reduced below the effective level. Instruments etc. immersed in disinfectant solutions must be dry.

Not only is the disinfectant rendered ineffective by dilution, a stage may be reached where immersion, far from producing disinfection, can actually infect the solution. Articles subsequently immersed for disinfection may thus become infected. This applies particularly to infection by such organisms as the tubercle bacillus which have a high resistance to chemical disinfectants in any case.

e) Temperature. Most disinfectants are more effective at higher temperatures.

f) Acidity/alkalinity. Some disinfectants are more active in alkaline solution whilst others are more effective at acid pH (see Appendix 2). The pH at which they are **stable** (i.e. not unduly subject to deterioriation with time) is not necessarily that at which they have the greatest disinfectant effect.

Such substances are supplied and stored at their stable pH. They need to be 'activated' before use by adjusting their pH to the optimum. A buffer is normally included in the activating solution to ensure that the pH remains within the desired range. Instructions relating to preparing the activated solution must be followed exactly so that the correct pH and buffering effect are attained otherwise the effectiveness of the product may be impaired.

g) **Inactivation**. Disinfectants may lose effectiveness for various reasons. Many are inactivated by the presence of organic matter such as tissue debris, dried blood, faeces, vomit etc. This is another good reason for cleaning all objects destined for sterilisation or disinfection. Some are inactivated by dilution with hard water, whilst others, such as the quaternary ammonium compounds, are inactivated by soaps.

Most disinfectants progressively lose their effectiveness with age, the rate varying from one substance to another. They are supplied in a relatively stable condition but dilution or activation often produces a much less stable product. Preparations must *never* be used beyond their expiry date. Such time-expired products present a double risk. Their efficacy cannot be relied upon and in such a state they can become infected and be a source of infection as described above.

TESTS FOR EFFECTIVENESS OF DISINFECTANTS

These are not of great importance to readers but it is useful to know that they exist since reference to them may be made in manufacturers' literature, journal articles, etc.

They are usually based on the effectiveness of various dilutions of the disinfectant on a given organism. This is compared with that of a standard such as a solution of phenol of specified strength. In some cases organic matter is added to relate the result more closely to probable working conditions. Early ones were the Rideal–Walker (RW) and Chick–Martin (CM) tests, whilst more recently the Kelsey and Kelsey–Sykes tests have been introduced.

AVAILABLE SUBSTANCES

There are several ways in which disinfectant and antiseptic substances might be classified; probably the simplest is to group

together those which are chemically similar. This method will be used and the groups examined in alphabetical order. They are:
- alcohols
- aldehydes
- diguanides
- halogens
- phenols
- quaternary ammonium compounds ('QAC's or 'Quats')
- QAC/diguanide combinations
- miscellaneous

The reader may not recognise some of these names but the actual compounds will usually be familiar.

ALCOHOLS

The alcohols are a large range of chemically-related substances whose correct names normally end in the letters 'ol'. Their older names are usually more familiar so these will be used. Only three are important here: methyl, ethyl and isopropyl alcohols, otherwise known as methanol, ethanol and isopropanol.

The word 'alcohol' in colloquial use refers to ethyl alcohol. There are heavy duties on alcoholic drinks and these are really duties on the alcohol content. They also apply to ethyl alcohol itself so that pure ('absolute') ethyl alcohol is an extremely expensive substance.

Because ethyl alcohol is such a useful substance there are various ways of avoiding duty. The simplest is to use one of the 'denatured' preparations which are mixtures of alcohol with other substances to render them undrinkable. The commonest of these are surgical spirit, mineralised methylated spirit and industrial methylated spirit (IMS).

Industrial methylated spirit (IMS) is alcohol to which 5 per cent of methyl alcohol has been added. Since it is not available for sale to the general public the methyl alcohol alone is sufficient to denature it but its sale is carefully controlled. (Methyl alcohol is poisonous, causing blindness and death.)

Mineralised methylated spirit contains, in addition, mineral naphtha (a paraffin-like substance), pyridine and a purple dye. It is not merely poisonous but extremely unpleasant to drink and the taste cannot be concealed by added flavours. This is the normal household 'methylated spirit', used for burning etc. There are few restrictions on its sale and it can be bought freely. It is not suitable for medical purposes and dilution with water gives a cloudy product.

Surgical spirit is a mixture of IMS, castor oil etc, and intended to be used undiluted as a lotion. It is freely saleable.

IMS is intended for industrial purposes as a solvent and is not available for sale to the general public. It is, however, available for business use and the procedure for obtaining supplies is as follows.

A permit is issued by the local Customs and Excise officer whose address is in the telephone directory. This officer should be contacted and the proposed use explained to him. He will describe the regulations and issue a permit. The permit is produced at the local pharmacy to obtain supplies and must be shown on each occasion. IMS is quite inexpensive, much the same price as mineralised methylated spirit.

It was noted earlier that the presence of water was essential to the effectiveness of disinfectants.

At one time bacteria used for assessment of anti-bacterial activity were in a dry form. When alcohol was used against these test organisms the pure substance did not appear to have much activity whilst mixtures of 70 per cent and 30 per cent water seemed to be the most effective. Many older books therefore state that alcohol should always be used at 70 per cent strength and never undiluted.

In fact, provided that the organisms are not in a very dry state stronger solutions can be used and in certain circumstances may be slightly more effective. Nevertheless it has become the custom to use 70 per cent alcohol for these purposes and cover is thereby provided where insufficient water is present.

A product of approximately this strength can be made by mixing three parts of IMS with one part of boiled and cooled water. These rather unexpected quantities are used because IMS is made from 95 per cent alcohol. Alternatively, most pharmacists would be prepared to supply it ready diluted, although they would need to obtain permission from Customs and Excise to do so. This permission should be readily forthcoming and is not required when the ultimate user prepares the dilution. For convenience, make up a stock supply of the 70 per cent mixture, and keep a separate small bottle for day-to-day use. The 70 per cent mixture is quite stable and should be stored in a closed bottle in a cool place.

Never pour the in-use solution back into the stock-bottle. Should the in-use solution have become contaminated, this would contaminate the whole supply.

Replace the in-use solution daily. If the solution may have been further diluted or if it ceases to be an absolutely clear liquid replace it at once.

An in-use solution is one from which stocks are drawn for immediate use – for moistening a swab, for example. It does *not* refer to a solution used for the soak-disinfection of instruments and alcohol is *never* used repeatedly for this purpose. If alcohol is used in an emergency for the soak-disinfection of, say, hairdressers' scissors the solution may be used *once only* and must then be discarded. The container should then be thoroughly cleaned with detergent, rinsed and allowed to dry. Preferably, after cleaning, it may be filled with a chlorine disinfectant (see page 79), left filled overnight, rinsed, and allowed to dry. Ideally it may be sterilised in an autoclave and allowed to dry.

Fatal infections have occurred when alcohol has been used repeatedly for soak disinfection and has become contaminated with *Clostridium* spores. Such soak-disinfection use of alcohol should *never* form part of a routine disinfection procedure. These comments also apply to such use of alcoholic solutions of chlorhexidine (see page 78).

If the volume of the in-use solution is planned carefully it should be possible to use it entirely in one or two days so that it is replaced as frequently as this. Wash out the in-use bottle with boiled water and dry it before refilling. This procedure applies to all such in-use solutions described in the following pages.

Isopropyl alcohol is rather more expensive than IMS, similar in disinfectant properties, but slightly more effective. It is preferred by some workers. Customs and Excise permission is not needed to buy it and supplies can be obtained from retail pharmacies.

As with IMS, it should be diluted to approximately 70 per cent by mixing three parts of isopropyl alcohol with one part of boiled and cooled water. The solution is used in the same way as diluted IMS, and with the same precautions.

A form of alcohol valuable to readers of this book is the ready-for-use alcohol swab.

Small pieces of tissue or cotton wool impregnated with 70 per cent IMS or isopropyl alcohol, or a solution of chlorhexidine, are available commercially in dispensers of 100–200 swabs. These are a clean and convenient means of using alcohols as an alternative to moistening swabs as required. There are no legal restrictions on their sale.

Methyl alcohol is a much weaker disinfectant than ethyl or isopropyl and is therefore not used for this purpose. It is mentioned above solely to identify it as a denaturant for ethyl alcohol.

The action of alcohols is bactericidal, producing a rapid kill of vegetative forms of bacteria. Bacterial spores are, however, resistant.

As noted above, fatal infections with *Clostridia* have been reported where instruments have been 'sterilised' by immersion in alcohol which had become contaminated with spores. This example serves to emphasise the limitations of such procedures where heat sterilisation should have been used.

The virucidal effect of alcohols is very limited but varies somewhat with the type of virus.

Several workers have commented on its inadequacy against HBV. However, in recent papers by Boyd *et al.* and Kobayashi *et al.* (see page 42) using chimpanzees as test animals, success against this virus was reported. One of these workers used 80 per cent ethyl alcohol and the other 70 per cent isopropyl alcohol. Spire *et al.* (see page 42) reported that 25 per cent ethyl alcohol was apparently effective against HIV.

The absence of reverse transcriptase activity (see page 23) was used as an indication of effectiveness.

Despite this evidence, alcohols should not be regarded as virucidal, especially towards HBV. The infectivity of this organism is so high that sterilisation is the only acceptable procedure for first-line equipment such as needles and other sharps. It does, however, emphasise the value of alcohols as disinfectants against a wide range of potential pathogens.

ALDEHYDES

These are members of another large group of chemical compounds characterised by the presence of a —CHO group. They are very active chemically and some are extremely efficient disinfectants.

The chemical activity leads to one disadvantage – in some circumstances their molecules combine to form **polymers**. This is known as **polymerisation**. The polymers have no disinfectant activity and effectiveness is lost progressively as polymerisation takes place. Their useful life is therefore limited.

The two aldehydes most commonly used for disinfection are formaldehyde and glutaraldehyde.

Formaldehyde
This is a gas, soluble in water, and usually occurs as a 40 per cent aqueous solution, containing methyl alcohol to retard polymerisation. This solution is known as 'formalin' and is usually diluted 2–20 per cent with water before use.

It is biocidal, being effective against bacteria, animal viruses and fungi. At temperatures above 40 °C bacterial spores are destroyed. It is highly irritant to tissues and eyes, and must not be applied to the skin. Its use is limited to special applications such as destroying anthrax spores on wool, hair, hide, etc., on a commercial basis. The gas is used to disinfect rooms, bedding, etc.

Glutaraldehyde
This is probably the most valuable disinfecting agent available. It occurs commercially as an amber coloured liquid of acid pH. In this form it is relatively stable.

For disinfectant use, the traditional product (Cidex) is a 2 per cent aqueous acid solution. This is only moderately active but is stable with a long shelf-life. A separate activator is supplied. The addition of the activator produces an alkaline buffered solution at about pH 8. This is a highly active disinfectant but unfortunately it polymerises readily. It has very a limited shelf life of 14 days (or 28 days in its 'long life' form) after which it must be discarded.

Since the expiry of the original patent, several new formulations of glutaraldehyde have appeared on the market. These will be discussed at the end of this section. For present purposes and throughout this book, the term 'glutaraldehyde' will be taken to mean the 2 per cent activated alkaline solution.

Glutaraldehyde will kill vegetative bacteria, including the more resistant ones, in less than a minute, and *M. tuberculosis* and most other viruses in less than 10 minutes. Bacterial spores, including those of the highly resistant *B. subtilis*, are killed in less than three hours.

One worker describes it as 'chemosteriliser'. Although sporicidal, at three hours it takes much longer to kill spores than does autoclaving. The term 'high level germicide' rather than sterilising agent has therefore been proposed for it. Since it is not customary to accept any cold disinfectant as a sterilising agent, this seems a useful description.

Glutaraldehyde also possesses high fungicidal activity.

There are adverse effects of glutaraldehyde – although much less irritant than formaldehyde it is classed as slightly irritant to the skin and severely irritant to the eyes. Skin sensitivity varies with individuals and allergic contact dermatitis has been recorded. Skin contact with the solution should be avoided, and rubber gloves used by those who are unduly sensitive. It is *imperative* to avoid contact with the eyes. Any accidental splashing in the eye requires *immediate* washing out with copious quantities of water and medical attention without delay.

Careless handling of the solution in the presence of clients could involve a risk of their being splashed. Should this occur in the eye, the above action must be taken at once.

Risks to clients can be minimised by forethought in arranging treatment trolleys etc. Only small amounts of potent substances should be kept on such trolleys. They should be placed so that clients are unlikely to knock them over. To have them below the level of the seated client's face is a sensible precaution.

Instruments made from plastic or rubber will absorb some glutaraldehyde and they should be wiped, rinsed and dried before use. For instruments used by readers, absorption is not likely to be a problem.

As with all solutions, dilution will reduce effectiveness, and care must be taken to avoid introducing water into the solution on wet instruments. Reasonable amounts of organic matter do not affect its activity but contamination should be avoided. Any solution displaying visible contamination such as slight cloudiness or specks of solid matter should be discarded. The maker's recommendations about the effective life of the solutions (14 or 28 days) should be followed closely and the product discarded immediately the expiry date is attained.

Although the solution is said to be safe for most metals, rubber and plastics, the writer's experience is that small thin plastic items may swell or distort slightly when kept in the solution. This is not normally a problem but should be borne in mind as a possibility.

The patents relating to the disinfectant actions of glutaraldehyde have now expired. New formulations aimed at reducing the problems associated with 2 per cent activated alkaline solutions are now appearing on the market. One such preparation, Sporicidin, contains sodium phenate. It is used at much greater dilution than the earlier 2 per cent solution and is claimed to have a life after activation of 30 days. Despite the further dilution it is said to remain an adequate disinfectant, although needing longer immersion in the more extreme cases. Other products are intended for use without activation. Some are supplied as stable solutions of acid pH. They may contain additional substances such as surface active agents (see page 81) to improve their efficacy at such pH. Others are recommended to be used at elevated temperature such as 60 °C, or used in ultrasonic equipment.

The timid reader may have come to the conclusion that glutaraldehyde has too many problems. Professional people accept that most things which are worthwhile have some disadvantages. To provide the best service for clients, risks must be appraised and problems accepted. What is important is to be aware of the disadvantages and act responsibly to minimise or eliminate them.

Finally, a brief summary on the use of glutaraldehyde.
- Time of immersion is just as important as sterilising time in an autoclave. Such timing should always be done by a clock.
- Follow directions about life and preparation of solutions and adhere to them strictly. Always record the expiry or preparation date on the label when making up solutions.
- Discard and replace any solution which shows the slightest sign of deterioration.
- Handle products with great care.

DIGUANIDES

The best known member of this group is **chlorhexidine** (Hibitane – ICI). It has a high level of antibacterial activity, low toxicity, and tends to bind to the skin.

With repeated application a lasting bactericidal effect is built up and it is widely used for skin disinfection. It can be applied both to the operator's hands and to the patient's skin in the area to be treated.

Chlorhexidine is bactericidal at high dilution but aqueous solutions are only bacteriostatic towards the tubercle bacillus. If it is considered important to eliminate this organism, aqueous solutions should be heat-sterilised. The alcohol in alcoholic solutions largely overcomes this problem and alcoholic solutions are therefore preferable.

Yeasts are inhibited by chlorhexidine but otherwise its fungistatic effect is variable.

Some enveloped viruses are inhibited but its effect on viruses is limited. Again the alcoholic solution may have a slightly wider anti-viral spectrum due to the additive effect of the alcohol.

Bacterial spores are also resistant.

Hibiscrub (ICI), a 4 per cent solution of chlorhexidine with detergents, is a valuable preparation for pre-operative hand-washing. Hibisol (ICI), a 0.5 per cent solution in isopropyl alcohol, is a useful skin disinfectant. For immediate effect Hibisol is no more effective than alcohol alone but repeated use – say, between clients – ensures a build-up of chlorhexidine on the skin providing an ongoing cover which could not be provided by alcohol alone.

There is also an aerosol product, Dispray 2 (Stuart Pharmaceuticals) – a solution in 70 per cent IMS for disinfection of hard surfaces such as working tops, treatment chairs, couches etc.

Apart from these products a range of preparations combining chlorhexidine with cetrimide is available and will be discussed later in this chapter.

The incidence of skin irritation or sensitivity with chlorhexidine is rare although some persons may find that repeated use of alcoholic solutions may have a drying effect on the skin. Chlorhexidine is incompatible with ordinary soap. If the hands are washed with soap and water and subsequently treated with a chlorhexidine hand disinfectant they should be well rinsed and dried before the chlorhexidine product is applied.

As mentioned earlier, solutions may become contaminated with tubercle bacillus or spores of organisms such as *Clostridia*. Such solutions should not ordinarily be used for soak-disinfection of instruments due to this contamination risk, but note the comments under alcohol, (page 73).

HALOGENS

There are five substances in this group but only two are used for disinfectant purposes – **chlorine** and **iodine**.

Chlorine

Chlorine is a poisonous, highly pungent and irritating yellowish gas. It can be used in specialised equipment to disinfect water by being dissolved in it. For most purposes compounds containing chlorine, especially **calcium** and **sodium hypochlorites** are used. These chlorine compounds are assessed in terms of 'parts per million' of 'available chlorine'. This theoretical figure is used as a measure of disinfectant effect.

Quite low concentrations of chlorine will kill most bacteria although the tubercle bacillus is resistant except at elevated temperatures. Bacterial spores are moderately resistant whilst viruses are moderately sensitive.

The hypochlorites are amongst the cheapest disinfectant materials available. Even when 'stabilised' they are very unstable compounds and are readily inactivated by organic matter. They tend to be corrosive and so are unsuitable for treating metal instruments. They are, however, particularly useful for disinfecting plastic, glass, ceramic and glaze-enamelled surfaces including floors, working tops, dishes, bowls, sanitary fittings, etc.

The commonest commercially available products are Milton and household bleaches such as Domestos and Chloros. Milton is a stabilised 1 per cent solution of sodium hypochlorite. It should be used as directed on the pack.

A 10 per cent (one ounce or two tablespoonfuls in half a pint of water) solution of Domestos is excellent for wiping over surfaces to disinfect them. The dilute solution is unstable and should be freshly prepared each day, but the product is so cheap that this is no hardship.

There are many other chlorine-based compounds available, notably the **chloramines**. Their advantage usually lies in stability or convenience in handling but otherwise they have no real advantages over the very inexpensive bleaches described above.

Iodine

This is a purplish-brown crystalline solid, slightly soluble in water. It is more soluble in alcoholic or aqueous solutions of potassium iodide ('tincture of iodine'). These stain the skin brown and occasionally cause severe skin reactions.

There are also iodine compounds available (e.g. iodophores) which do not stain or irritate the skin. The iodophores are usually combined with surface-active agents thus offering a detergent/disinfectant effect (e.g. Betadine and other preparations of povidone iodine).

Iodine preparations are biocidal to almost all pathogenic micro-organisms. Exposure times required for a kill vary widely, especially for viruses and bacterial spores. Against HBV they appear to be less effective than 2 per cent activated glutaraldehyde. As with chlorine, the activity of iodine products is reduced by organic matter.

Iodine preparations are used mainly for skin disinfection and iodophores have largely replaced iodine/iodide solutions for this purpose.

PHENOLS

These are substances related to phenol (carbolic acid) which was the early antiseptic used by Lister in surgery. Phenol itself is now little used as a general disinfectant. Various related compounds such as the cresols and xylenols are used in products such as Lysol and Izal for disinfection of toilets, excreta, etc. They are little inactivated by organic matter (hence their value in disinfecting faeces) and are bactericidal against Gram-positive and Gram-negative organisms although acid-fast bacilli and spores are resistant.

Chlorxylenol, the active principle of Dettol is effective against Gram-positive organisms but less so against Gram-negatives. It is highly inactivated by organic matter but has the advantage of low toxicity so that it can be used on skin and tissues.

Hexachlorophane is a weak bactericide but a useful bacteriostatic. Like chlorxylenol, it is effective against Gram-positive organisms. Combined with detergents, it has been used as a pre-operative surgical scrub where its effectiveness against *Staph. aureus* is a great advantage. It has fallen somewhat into disrepute since in infants repeated exposure, with absorption, may result in a build-up with possible brain-damage and death.

QUATERNARY AMMONIUM COMPOUNDS

These are often abbreviated to QACs or Quats. They are **surface active** compounds and are especially valuable as **cationic detergents**. A short digression is necessary to explain these terms.

Soaps and other detergents are surface active agents – they change the surface tension of water, improving its 'wetting power'. They facilitate the removal of oily substances which would not normally mix with water. The synthetic detergents (a detergent is, of course, something which facilitates washing) are grouped into three classes: anionic, cationic and non-ionic. All are excellent cleansing agents but the cationic and anionic detergents inactivate each other so must not be mixed or used at the same time. Cationic detergents such as Quats are also inactivated by soaps.

The biocidal/biostatic properties of the Quats have been widely investigated. They are probably best considered as bacteriostatic. Spores, many viruses and acid-fast bacilli are resistant, even at high concentration.

Probably the best-known product in this group is cetrimide (Cetavlon – ICI).

QAC/DIGUANIDE COMBINATIONS

By combining the detergent action of cetrimide with the bactericidal activity of chlorhexidine an enhanced preparation is obtained.

The commercial product Savlon (ICI) is such a combination. It is widely used as a surgical scrub, for pre-operative skin treatment and for cleaning wounds, etc. Aqueous solutions may become infected with the resistant tubercle bacillus and with some *Pseudomonas* species so that they are unsuitable for soak-disinfection of instruments.

MISCELLANEOUS DISINFECTANTS AND ANTISEPTICS

Apart from the above groups of substances, many others have been used. These include dyes such as the acridines, crystal violet (gentian violet), brilliant green, malachite green, etc. Also 8-hydroxyquinoline, β-propiolactone, various mercury compounds and many others.

The substances detailed in this chapter, however, are those most widely used and available at the time of writing and from them a selection can readily be made.

SUMMARY

In this chapter, a wide range of substances for use as disinfectants or antiseptics has been considered. Many less well known but deserving substances have been omitted. Pointers as to possible uses have been included and these will be examined in greater detail in Chapter 7.

CHAPTER 7

Design of hygienic procedures for use in a practice

So far in this book the general features of the organisms which cause disease and the conditions for which they are responsible have been discussed briefly. The diseases with which readers' work may be concerned were then examined in greater detail. The various methods, physical and chemical, of preventing infection, especially those which may be useful in practice were then outlined.

In this chapter this information is brought together to consider what anti-infective measures would be most suitable for the clinic or salon situation. The illustration on page 84 shows a clinic or salon in which there are several obvious hazards and readers should be able to identify some of these, even before reading this chapter. When you have read Chapter 7, look again at this drawing and list the faults you can find. Compare your results with the list on page 120.

BASIC CONSIDERATIONS

Several factors must be taken into account if the most suitable methods are to be chosen:

- Nature of the operation
  a) known risks, as indicated by published literature, personal experience, etc.

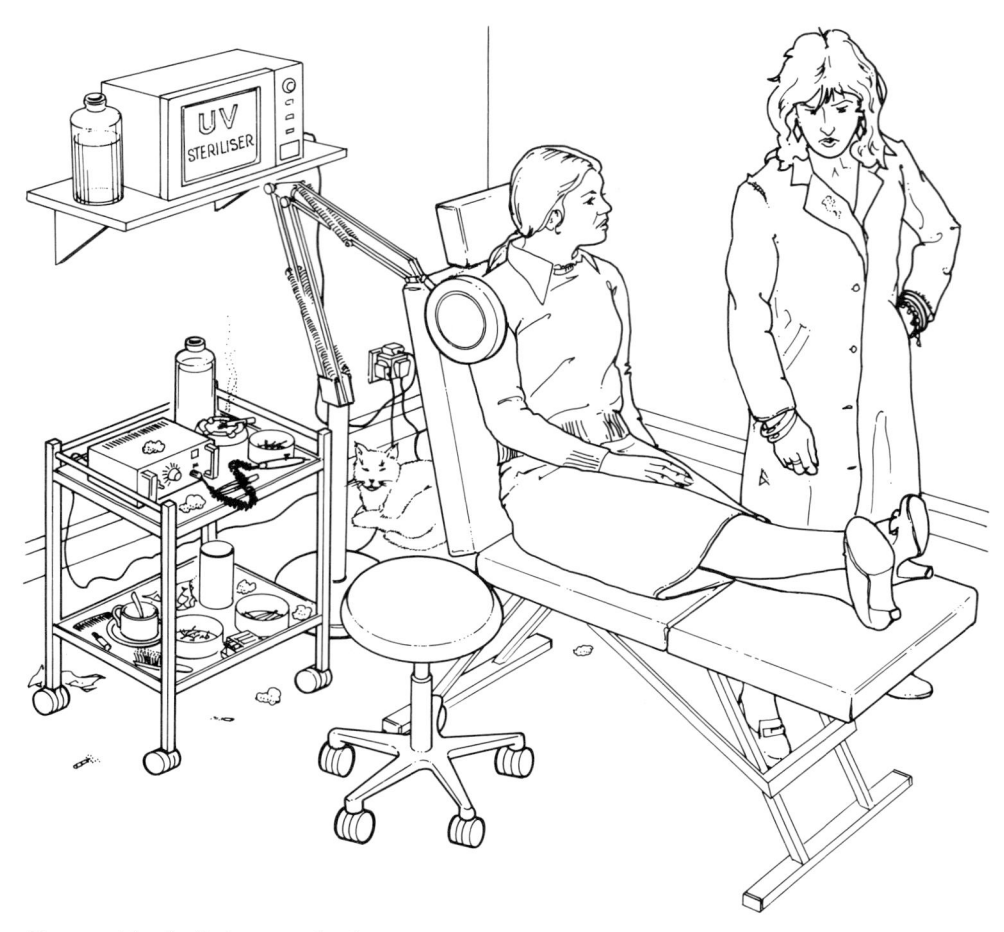

Not an ideal clinic or salon!

    b) whether the skin is pierced, intentionally or accidentally, with sufficient frequency to constitute a risk
    c) whether bleeding is usual or likely to occur
    d) anticipated infections.

- Equipment used
  a) disposable
  b) re-usable
  c) materials from which it is made
  d) its proximity in use to the treated area and, especially, if it is likely to become contaminated with blood or patient-secretions.

- Legal requirements
- Type of patient
  a) male
  b) female
  c) both.
- Materials and methods available
- Working environment
  a) premises
  b) general fittings
  c) sanitary arrangements
  d) floor and wall coverings.
- Disposal of waste

These will now be examined in turn.

NATURE OF THE OPERATION

a) Known risks
Treatments usually involve the skin and hair and in the past the perceived risks were bacteriological or parasitic. In most cases they were more a nuisance than a threat to life. Louse infections of the scalp are much less common than in earlier days and whilst the possibility of bacterial infection remains, virus infections are now the main problem.

Although the risk of hepatitis has presumably always existed it is only in recent years that the importance of skin-piercing cosmetic operations in its spread has been recognised. The increasing risk of HIV infection reinforces the need for suitable precautions and it is towards these two virus infections that most effort must be directed.

Professional organisations should keep their members informed of developments. Publications such as this book provide the background knowledge for an understanding of these.

b) Is the skin pierced?
In some procedures such as tattooing, ear-piercing and acupuncture, piercing the skin is an inevitable and fundamental part of the operation. In the case of electrolysis for hair removal it does not normally occur, but may happen accidentally. When used for treating spider veins, broken capillaries and warts of course,

electrolysis also inevitably involves skin-piercing. In hairdressing, accidental cutting with scissors, or more probably with razors may occur.

c) Does bleeding take place?
Where this does occur, risks are substantially increased. The operator's hands and anything he touches subsequently such as telephones, appointment books, pens and pencils, coins, work surfaces, etc., become contaminated and the infection can be spread to the next client.

d) Anticipated infections
As indicated above, the most important problem-infections which might be met are viral, HBV and HIV. Both are transmitted primarily by cross-infection through transfer of body-fluids, especially blood. In addition, remember the long survival time of HBV on inert surfaces. Whilst HIV is very unlikely to have such a long survival time, some experts are claiming it may survive several days on infected needles. Fortunately, methods used to control these viruses will normally also control any bacterial infections which could be a problem.

EQUIPMENT USED

a) Disposable
Increasingly, the tendency is to use disposable equipment whenever possible, especially in the high-risk parts of the equipment which may actually pierce the skin. Thus disposable needles and razors, supplied sterile, used once only and disposed of safely, are the ideal for many operators and patients.

Care must always be taken with such equipment that it is not infected by careless handling. Frequently the pack is designed so that the instrument can be inserted into the equipment whilst the most sensitive area is still protected. Where it is necessary to use forceps, for example to insert needles into needle holders they must be sterile, kept so, and resterilised at least daily by a heat-method.

It will probably be necessary to use forceps to remove needles from their holders after use. It is very difficult to avoid these forceps making contact with the contaminated part of the used needle and so becoming infected themselves.

Such forceps are termed 'dirty' and are retained solely for this purpose. They must also be sterilised at least daily. They are probably best kept between use in 2 per cent activated glutaraldehyde in a container retained for them alone. They should be dried on a disposable tissue before use.

b) Re-usable equipment

Re-usable needles etc., must *never* be used again on a second client without being resterilised.

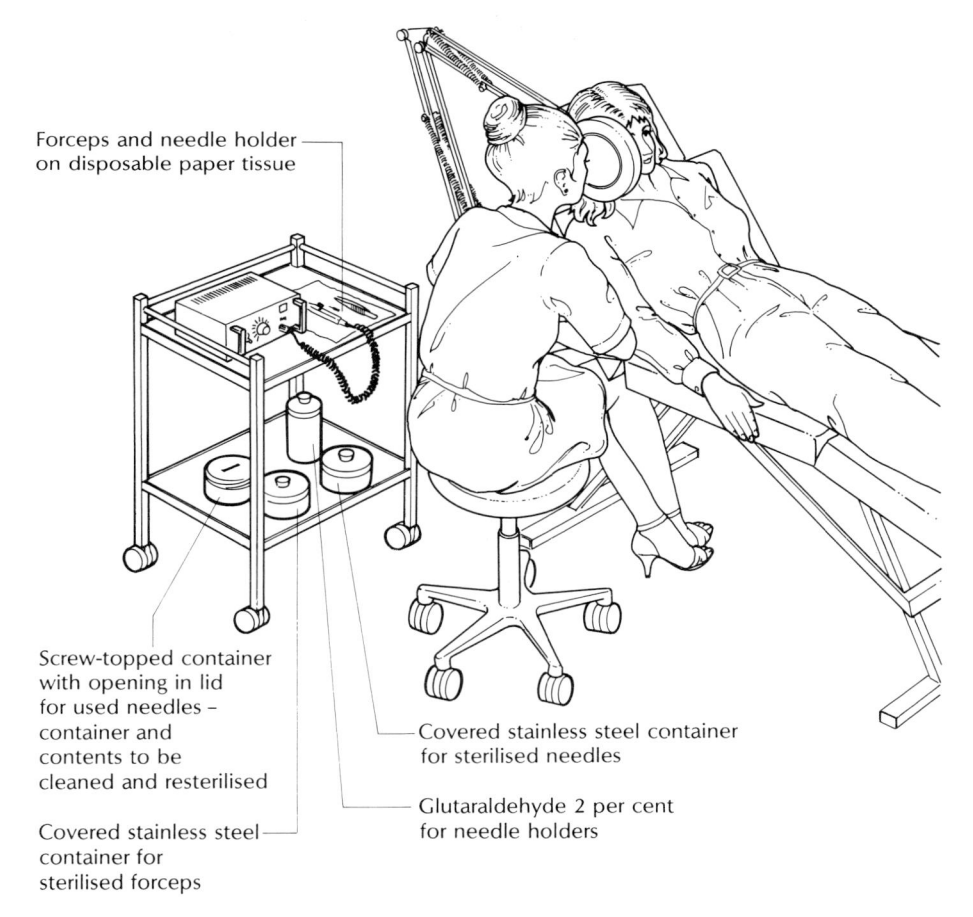

- Forceps and needle holder on disposable paper tissue
- Screw-topped container with opening in lid for used needles – container and contents to be cleaned and resterilised
- Covered stainless steel container for sterilised forceps
- Covered stainless steel container for sterilised needles
- Glutaraldehyde 2 per cent for needle holders

Electrolysis equipment. Note that the minimum of equipment is kept on the treatment trolley and that chemicals are in closed containers on the bottom shelf. The containers for sterile and used needles will not be confused – the one for used needles has an opening in the lid.

After use they are removed with 'dirty' forceps as above and placed in a leak-proof and sterilisable box with a cover. At least daily the needles, etc., and their storage boxes and covers must be cleaned and sterilised. Care should be taken that their storage boxes cannot be confused with those used for sterile needles.

Before leaving the subject of needles, the risks to the operator from used needles must again be emphasised.'Needle-stabs' are an occupational hazard and, if the needles are infected, can readily infect the operator. Every care must be taken to avoid them, and always to handle such needles with forceps is probably the simplest precaution.

c) Materials from which equipment is made
The materials from which equipment is made will govern the method of sterilisation or disinfection which can be applied to it.

In sterilising disposable materials on a commercial basis, as seen, a wider range of methods is available. Where resterilising is required in the clinic or salon, the range of methods is limited. As has been emphasised frequently in this book, heat is the only acceptable method and moist heat is preferred. Where materials cannot be heat sterilised, chemical disinfection will be required, using the most effective disinfectant available.

d) Proximity in use
Equipment in use will vary in its proximity to the client and therefore in its risk of becoming contaminated by body-fluids such as blood. For example, in electrolysis the needle is always inserted into a hair-follicle. Of all the equipment used, it is in closest proximity to the patient. Nothing less than sterility is therefore acceptable for needles. Working tops, however, are more remote from the patient. Although they may become infected, possibly from the operator's hands, they represent a much smaller risk than needles. Good quality disinfection, frequently applied, is acceptable for them.

LEGAL REQUIREMENTS

In the UK, the most important legal requirements at the time of writing, are the by-laws and registration requirements made by local authorities under the Local Government (Miscellaneous Provisions) Act, 1982.

This Act empowers local authorities to require registration of persons wishing to perform tattooing, acupuncture, ear-piercing and electrolysis in their area, and their premises. A certificate of registration must be issued and displayed in the premises to which it relates.

The authority may also make by-laws relating to hygiene, sterilisation and cleanliness in registered premises and these must also be displayed (Chapter 30, Sections 14.7 and 15.7). Whilst the authority is free to make any by-laws it wishes, in almost every case it adopts the 'model by-laws' and these are reproduced in full in Chapter 9.

The by-laws etc., are enforced by the authority's Department of Environmental Health and for further information in any area this Department should be contacted.

It cannot be too strongly emphasised that any certificate of registration as described above does not in any way indicate the competence of the operator to carry out the work for which he or she is registered. Advertisements of services should never carry statements such as 'registered with the local authority' or 'approved by the local authority' where this could be construed by a reader to imply approval of the operator's competence. Indeed, until by-laws have been made, premises inspected and methods approved, a certificate of registration does not even indicate that satisfactory hygiene measures are in force. Many enlightened authorities, realising this, are rewording their certificates of registration to make these points clear.

The model by-laws impose certain specific requirements and these are indicated later in this chapter.

TYPE OF PATIENT

Disease is no respecter of persons. Nevertheless, the sex, age and behaviour of clients may be relevant to their potential to spread disease. This is less likely to be the case with HBV infection although it can be transmitted sexually and the promiscuous are therefore perhaps more likely to be carriers.

In the case of AIDS, in the UK at the time of writing, infection is much more common in men than in women, and especially amongst practising promiscuous homosexuals. This male dominance is unlikely to continue as heterosexual spread becomes more common.

In an electrolysis practice, where clients are predominantly women, it may be a sound business decision to treat women only or to avoid the known promiscuous of either sex. Such a policy cannot be a substitute for safe procedures but it may serve to make regular clients feel more comfortable.

The area in which the practice is situated may also influence policy. Remember that, at the time of writing, 77 per cent of the UK AIDS cases were in the London area with most of the remainder in other large centres of population. In deference to others, readers practising in such areas may wish to be selective in their choice of client. If high-risk clients are treated, certain times may be set aside for them, perhaps at the end of the working day. A complete set of equipment may be kept especially for their use and such inconvenience may well justify a higher charge.

MATERIALS AND METHODS AVAILABLE

In choosing equipment, an important consideration should be whether it can readily be sterilised. Something which can be autoclaved is always preferable.

Stainless steel is an ideal material whilst aluminium is also valuable. Mild steel is liable to rusting. This results not only in deterioration of appearance but in the formation of 'pits' which are difficult to clean.

Some plastics such as TPX can be autoclaved repeatedly, at any rate at 121 °C, without deterioration. Others may be deformed by such treatment. Dry heat sterilising temperatures are normally too high for plastics. Manufacturers should be able to confirm the suitability of their products for repeated autoclaving. No doubt, with increased interest in the subject, more thermostable materials will be used.

CHOICE OF WORKING ENVIRONMENT

The actual choice of premises for a business depends on commercial considerations but within the premises the arrangements will be influenced to some extent by the hygiene requirements.

Apart from obvious things such as accessibility, availability of toilet accommodation for clients and the like, the actual working area is the most important.

Washing facilities for operators, with a hot water supply on tap, so that an operator can wash her hands before each patient, are essential. These should preferably be in the working area or, immediately adjacent to it. Taps should be elbow or foot-controlled and disposable paper towels or hot-air driers should be installed. Cotton towels should not be used as they can be a source of re-infection.

Walls and floors should be capable of being cleaned and the premises should always be kept clean.

Hard washable floor surfaces are ideal from a cleanliness viewpoint, and for higher-risk procedures such as tattooing they are essential. For electrolysis and for most beauty work, carpets are acceptable and many people prefer them from an aesthetic point of view.

Work-tops, shelves, etc., in the working area should have a hard impervious surface such as plastic laminate, glass or stainless steel. As far as possible they should be free of odd corners where dirt can collect and which are difficult to clean. Such surfaces must be kept uncluttered and the number of items of equipment in use kept to a minimum.

Chairs and couches for clients, and stools etc. for operators, should have a smooth and impervious surface such as vinyl or other plastic and this should be kept in good repair. The model by-laws require that a couch has a disposable paper cover, renewed for each client. This is not required for chairs. A good guide is that where a client's bare skin comes into contact with a chair or couch surface, a paper cover should be used.

If possible it is always preferable that an appointments secretary or receptionist deals with telephone calls, payment and handling money, making appointments, etc. The operator is then not taken away from the clean working area. A single-handed operator should always bear in mind that she can readily infect other surfaces from possibly infected hands. This could be a source of future re-infection.

DISPOSAL OF WASTE

The model by-laws lay down requirements for the disposal of 'clinical waste' which could be infected.

Basically there are two types of waste, sharp objects such as disposable needles, razors etc., usually referred to as 'sharps', and swabs, dressings, paper coverings, gloves and the like. Used sharps are a particular hazard since they can penetrate the skin of any handler and infect them. The operator is not the only person at risk. Workers who handle waste subsequently must be protected.

Disposal arrangements can usually be made with the local authority cleansing department – most larger authorities have special arrangements for collection and disposal of clinical waste. Contact the Director of Cleansing or seek information from the local Environmental Health Officer. Alternatively, especially in more rural

Discard immediately after use

Discard immediately after use

Put closed box into sack when full

Empty into sack at least once a day

Removed for incineration

Disposal of clinical waste.

areas, local hospitals will have a waste-disposal arrangement and will often accept waste for incineration. The administrative department of the hospital should be able to make the arrangements.

'Sharps' are usually placed in a stout impervious box made of combustible material. Special sharps disposal systems are available commercially for hospital use but these are unnecessary for small scale users. Swabs, etc., are placed in an impervious pedal-bin with a plastic liner and the model by-laws require that this liner be changed at least every working day. Normally the disposal authority issues special plastic bags in which the filled bin liners are placed for collection. Usually the 'sharps' box and contents are placed in the same plastic bag. Bins should be cleaned out and disinfected regularly. All these clinical waste materials are disposed of by incineration.

DISINFECTION AND STERILISATION OF EQUIPMENT

In relation to equipment, the model by-laws state that, 'an operator shall ensure that any needle, metal instrument, or other item of equipment used in treatment is in a sterile condition and kept sterile until used. For resterilisable needles, in addition, after use needles are placed in a separate covered and leakproof box, emptied at least once per working day and then sterilised.'

For needles, only heat sterilisation is acceptable – either a bead steriliser, hot air oven or, preferably, an autoclave, should be used. As cheaper autoclaves become available, their use should become universal. Any other equipment which can be heat-sterilised should be treated in this way and this is where an autoclave becomes particularly valuable. Such equipment includes forceps, scissors, and the covered dishes for needles, etc. The latter should be stainless steel, or plastic suited to repeated autoclaving.

For items which cannot, by their nature, be heat sterilised, the best disinfectant is activated glutaraldehyde. Electrolysis needle-holders can be wiped thoroughly with 70 per cent alcohol (preferably isopropyl alcohol) and the chuck-end immersed in glutaraldehyde for an hour. Before re-use the holder should be dried, washed thoroughly in clean water, and re-dried for use. Paper tissues are suitable for drying.

Forceps are often needed to assemble apparatus, for example they are needed to insert and remove electrolysis needles in the holder-chucks. Two forceps will normally be used – a 'clean' pair for inserting needles and a 'dirty' pair for removing them after use. The greatest care is needed to differentiate between the two pairs. Ideally, when forceps have been used to remove used needles they should be placed in a covered leakproof box until the end of the day and then cleaned and sterilised. Rather than having to distinguish between dirty and clean forceps, one newly sterilised pair can be used for each client – to insert the needle into the holder and to remove it after treatment – and then put in the covered box for cleaning and sterilising at the end of the day.

A more practical way would be to wipe the dirty forceps and store them largely immersed in glutaraldehyde until the next use. They should then be cleaned and heat-sterilised at least daily. Great care should be taken to keep this glutaraldehyde container separate from all others and retain it only for this purpose. The glutaraldehyde should be changed frequently.

For wiping down worktops, which should be done frequently during the working day, chlorine preparations such as 10 per cent Domestos are ideal and should certainly be used at the end of the day. During the day it may be more convenient to use a swab moistened in 70 per cent alcohol, or a proprietary product such as Dispray 2 (an alcoholic solution of chlorhexidine in an aerosol). Similar treatment can be used for the plastic surfaces of chairs, and couches. The aerosol product is especially useful as the fine spray penetrates corners in upholstery etc.

Work surfaces that are used by the operator during treatment may be covered with a paper tissue or towel, renewed for each client.

A final point to remember in relation to needles is that the operator should *never* test them on himself. This practice is dangerous both to operator and client. If it is necessary to check, for instance, the functioning of an electrolysis machine, the operator should regard himself as a new client. A new needle and holder are used for the test, reverting to the original equipment when returning to the patient.

ANTISEPTICS FOR USE ON TREATED AREAS OF CLIENTS

To reduce the possibility of bacterial infection, the client's skin may be cleaned before and after the treatment. A spirit swab (a piece of cotton wool, moistened in 70 per cent alcohol) can be used. Other lotions, and especially antibiotic preparations are *not* recommended. The treated area should be kept dry during the actual treatment.

When applying lotions etc., particular care must be taken not to infect the container by re-moistening a used swab. Operators should cultivate the habit of moistening the swab, applying it, *discarding it in the waste-bin*, and then starting again with a new swab if a further application is required. The cycle of moisten swab, apply it and discard it should be carefully developed.

PERSONAL CLEANLINESS AND PROTECTION FOR OPERATORS

All operators should have a high standard of personal cleanliness. Nails should be well-trimmed and jewellery about the hands and wrists should be minimal. Clean overalls should be worn, with short sleeves, the forearms being bare. The wrists of long sleeves are extremely likely to become infected in brushing over the client's skin.

Hands should be washed between clients, preferably with a chlorhexidine containing detergent. Chlorhexidine creams and especially alcoholic solutions are also valuable for the operator's hands.

Wounds and open sores on the operator's hands, or anywhere not covered by clothing, should always be covered with a suitable dressing. This serves a dual purpose. They may be a source of infection to the client or a point at which infection from a client may enter the operator's blood-stream. 'Weeping' wounds, especially recent burns, are particularly prone to infection. Dressings must be changed frequently, especially if they become contaminated with a client's blood or body fluids.

Earlier in this chapter, emphasis was laid on the importance of avoiding 'needle-stick' injuries when handling needles. It is most important to avoid any contamination by the client's blood or tissue fluids where these could conceivably enter the operator's blood stream.

There are four common routes of such infection which operators must recognise and avoid:

- By mouth

    Particles of blood can easily get on to the operator's hands and, if he does not wash before eating, such particles could be transferred to his food and mouth. The model by-laws forbid food and drink in working areas and the greatest care should be taken in this respect.

- By splashing into the eyes

    If the operator's eyes are splashed with a client's blood, virus could enter his own blood stream. If such splashing occurs, the eyes must be washed out immediately with copious amounts of water. If the work involves a high risk of this event, protective glasses should be worn.

- Via open exposed wounds on the operator's hands etc.

    As mentioned above, these should always be covered by an impervious dressing. If the dressing becomes contaminated by the client's blood, remove it immediately, wash the wound thoroughly, dry it and apply a clean dressing. Do this without delay.

- By needle-stick injuries

    Remember the importance of avoiding needle-stick injuries from used, potentially infected needles.

    Operators should also note that if they inflict a needle-stick injury on themselves with a sterile needle, they could have infected it and it must not be used on a client until it has been resterilised.

Finally, readers should remember the trust their clients place in them to provide effective treatment and to do it without risk of disfigurement. Clients also trust that treatment will not infect them with a potentially fatal disease. Hygiene and sterilisation methods must be beyond reproach if their trust is not to be misplaced. This is a great responsibility.

CHAPTER 8

Self-examination questions

The purpose of this chapter is to help readers to check what has been learned. The questions can be attempted after reading each chapter or, if preferred, after reading the whole book. The answers are given in a separate section at the end of this chapter.

Where readers are uncertain of the answer, they should look again at the text. They will learn more readily by doing this than by going straight to the answers section.

The questions are in multiple-choice form. Readers preparing for an examination will probably find that this is the form it will take. For each question there are several possible answers and you should select the correct one(s). As always read and consider the question carefully – the answers are not always what they seem! The questions are arranged by chapter.

CHAPTER 1

1. Bacteria normally reproduce by
   A) meiosis
   B) reduction division
   C) binary fission.

2. The rigid shape of a bacterium is maintained by the
   A) protoplast
   B) cell wall
   C) flagella.

3. All bacteria have a well-defined nucleus.
   A) True
   B) False

4. Which TWO of the following genera are spore-forming bacteria?
   A) *Spirochaetes*
   B) *Haemophilus*
   C) *Clostridia*
   D) *Bacilli*
   E) *Corynebacterium*

5. Spores are important to us because
   A) they are a particularly rapid way of reproducing
   B) they are very resistant to sterilisation
   C) spore-forming organisms all cause mild skin infections.

6. Which of the following is essential for growth for all bacteria?
   A) Oxygen
   B) Carbon dioxide
   C) Hydrogen

7. For survival and growth, anaerobic bacteria
   A) must have oxygen
   B) can survive either in the presence or absence of oxygen
   C) need an atmosphere free of oxygen.

8. Cocci in shape are basically
   A) spherical
   B) rod-shaped
   C) spiral.

9. Straight, rod-shaped organisms are known as
   A) bacilli
   B) cocci
   C) spirillum.

10. Bacteria are stained for microscopical examination
    A) to help to identify them
    B) so that they can readily be seen.
    C) Both

11. Most cultures of human pathogenic bacteria are incubated at
    A) 20 °C
    B) 37 °C
    C) 42 °C

12. Pair the following statements (AB, AC, BC etc.).
    A) Exotoxins
    B) Endotoxins
    C) diffuse out of the cell-wall into the surrounding medium.
    D) are part of the bacterial cell and are only liberated when the cell is broken down.

13. Pair the following statements.
    A) *Staphylococcus*
    B) *Streptococcus*
    C) occur in chains.
    D) occur in clumps.

14. Which THREE of the following are common bacteria?
    A) *Salmonella*
    B) Fungi
    C) Protista
    D) *Proteus*
    E) Amoebae
    F) *Shigella*

CHAPTER 2

1. All viruses can be seen
   A) with the naked eye
   B) with a low-power optical microscope
   C) only with an electron microscope.

2. Viruses, when outside the cells which they infect,
   A) cannot survive
   B) cannot reproduce
   C) can mutate.

3. Which viruses possess an envelope?
   A) All
   B) Some
   C) None

4. Viruses can be cultured
   A) in the same media as bacteria
   B) only in tissue culture
   C) only in living cells.

5. Which of the following is not suitable for culturing viruses?
   A) Tissue cultures
   B) Hen egg embryos
   C) Nutrient agar

6. The AIDS virus is a member of which group?
   A) Poxviruses
   B) Retroviruses
   C) Herpesviruses

7. The AIDS virus is now known as
   A) HBV
   B) HAV
   C) HIV.

8. Hepatitis B is caused by
   A) HBV
   B) HAV
   C) HIV.

9. The hepatitis viruses are normally considered to be
   A) miscellaneous viruses
   B) Retroviruses
   C) Adenoviruses.

10. To which group of Fungi does *Candida albicans* belong?
    A) Yeast-like
    B) Filamentous
    C) Dimorphic

11. *Microsporum* causes
    A) thrush
    B) vaginitis
    C) ringworm of hair and scalp.

12. Athletes foot is commonly caused by
    A) *Epidermophyton*
    B) *Trichophyton*
    C) *Aspergillus*.

13. A saprophyte is an organism which
    A) is essentially pathogenic to animals
    B) lives on dead organic matter
    C) infects the conductive tissues of plants.

14. A Protist is a
    A) type of virus
    B) unicellular organism
    C) tropical worm.

15. Threadworms
    A) do not normally utilise an intermediate host
    B) alternate between humans and pigs
    C) alternate between domestic animals and humans.

16. Tapeworms belong to the genus
    A) *Tinea*
    B) *Taenia*
    C) *Trichinopolis*.

17. *Diphyllobothrium* is a tapeworm whose hosts are humans and
    A) pigs
    B) cattle
    C) fish.

18. Nits are the eggs of
    A) scabies mites
    B) thrush organisms
    C) head lice.

19. Lice feed by
    A) eating their way into the stratum corneum
    B) sucking the host's blood
    C) consuming the hairs amongst which they live.

CHAPTER 3

1. Which is the most likely source of human infection?
   A) Other animals
   B) Inanimate objects
   C) Other humans

2. Which is the most important route by which our work may spread disease?
   A) Infected food
   B) Droplet inhalation
   C) Cross-infection

3. A symptomless carrier is a person
   A) who knows he has a disease which is so mild that he does not bother treating it
   B) who is infected and will develop the disease but has not yet done so
   C) in whom the organisms exist but who shows no sign of the disease and is usually unaware of their presence.

4. Of the three common entry points for infection, which is the most important in readers' work?
   A) The respiratory tract
   B) The alimentary tract
   C) The skin or other surfaces

5. Organisms which live in or on the body but do not normally cause disease in healthy individuals are known as
   A) parasites
   B) pathogens
   C) commensals.

6. Which THREE of the following are part of the body's innate defence system against infection?
   A) T-lymphocytes
   B) Hair
   C) Saliva
   D) Antibodies
   E) Phagocytes
   F) Stomach secretions

7. Which TWO of the following are phagocytic?
   A) Lymphocytes
   B) Erythrocytes
   C) Polymorphs
   D) Macrophages
   E) Bacteriophages

8. Which of the above in question 7 is fundamentally different from the rest?

9. Antigens are substances which are
   A) secreted by bacteria
   B) capable of inducing the production of specific antibodies which will react with them, often neutralising them
   C) produced in response to antibodies.

10. Which TWO of the following are the most important diseases likely to be transmitted by skin-piercing and similar cosmetic procedures?
    A) HIV infection
    B) *Pneumocystis carinii* pneumonia
    C) Hepatitis A
    D) Kaposi's sarcoma
    E) Hepatitis B

11. By what route is hepatitis A most commonly spread?
    A) Skin piercing
    B) Faecally-infected water
    C) Inhaled droplet infection

12. How frequently does hepatitis B cause death?
    A) Very frequently
    B) Occasionally
    C) Very rarely

13. By what route is hepatitis B normally spread?
    A) Parenteral mixing of blood and related body fluids
    B) Faecally infected water
    C) Inhalation of infected droplets

14. What is the approximate incubation period of hepatitis B?
    A) 2–4 weeks
    B) 40–150 days
    C) More than 6 months

15. Which is the more likely to cause death?
    A) Hepatitis A
    B) Hepatitis B

16. Symptomless carriers of hepatitis B are
    A) quite common
    B) uncommon
    C) very unusual indeed.

17. AIDS is another name for HIV infections.
    A) True
    B) False

18. AIDS is an abbreviation for
    A) Acquired Infective Deficiency Syndrome
    B) Acquired Immune Deficiency Syndrome
    C) Auto-Immune Deficiency Syndrome

19. Which elements of the immune system are primarily damaged by HIV?
   A) Macrophages
   B) Polymorphs
   C) Certain T-lymphocytes

CHAPTER 4

1. Sterilisation means
   A) destruction of all living cells except bacterial spores
   B) destruction of all living cells except viruses
   C) destruction of all living micro-organisms.

2. Disinfection means
   A) destruction of all bacterial cells except spores
   B) the use of a substance which reduces the level of micro-organisms infection to one which is not harmful to health, without adversely affecting the quality of perishable goods
   C) the use of a bactericide which is never applied to the skin.

3. The effect of an antiseptic is to
   A) limit or prevent the harmful results of infection
   B) destroy all micro-organisms on the skin
   C) destroy all bacteria but not to be sporicidal.

4. A substance which is described as bactericidal only may not be suitable for clinic or salon purposes since
   A) the viruses HBV and HIV are not likely to be destroyed
   B) it will be severely irritant to the skin
   C) it will have no detergent effect.

5. Why is an antiseptic never described as 'virustatic'?
   A) No known antiseptic prevents the growth of viruses
   B) Viruses only reproduce in living cells
   C) Such a substance should properly be described as a disinfectant

CHAPTER 5

1. Do you regard 'cold sterilising solutions' as
   A) an efficient method of sterilisation
   B) likely to be efficient disinfectants
   C) potentially useful antiseptics.

2. Why are procedures which result in a rapid kill of organisms preferable to slower methods?
   A) They are less time-consuming
   B) Articles to be sterilised do not need cleaning
   C) The quicker the kill, the less likely that unkilled organisms will remain

3. Why should synthetic detergents be used in preference to soaps for cleaning?
   A) They are more gentle to the operator's hands
   B) They are less likely to cause deterioration of rubber and plastics
   C) They do not deposit hard scums when hard water is used.

4. Which of the following are TWO important reasons why articles to be sterilised or disinfected should be cleaned before use?
   A) The greater the number of organisms contaminating an article, the more likely that sterilisation etc. will be incomplete
   B) A shorter exposure time can safely be given if the articles are clean
   C) Many disinfectants render protein materials insoluble and more difficult to remove after treatment
   D) Some substances, e.g. oils and greases, will inhibit the penetration of steam to infected surfaces

5. Which is the preferred method of sterilisation for the small operator to use?
   A) Ethylene oxide
   B) Heat
   C) Irradiation

6. Which of the following is the preferred method of heat sterilisation, assuming that appropriate temperatures are reached?
   A) Saturated steam
   B) Superheated steam
   C) Dry Heat

7. What minimum temperature must be exceeded in dry heat sterilising to ensure killing spores
   A) 121 °C
   B) 134 °C
   C) 140 °C

8. What is the normal temperature range used in moist heat sterilisers?
   A) 105–15 °C
   B) 125–45 °C
   C) 121–34 °C

9. Why must air be eliminated from autoclaves used in sterilising?
   A) So that the correct temperature is reached for the working pressure attained
   B) To facilitate drying after the process is completed
   C) To reduce the likelihood of the pressure vessel bursting

10. Which TWO of the following time/temperature combinations are commonly used in autoclaving?
    A) 10 minutes at 121 °C
    B) 15 minutes at 121 °C
    C) 15 minutes at 126 °C
    D) 3 minutes at 134 °C

11. Why is a steam-jacket used on large commercial autoclaves?
    A) It reduces heat loss from the main chamber during sterilisation
    B) It reduces the likelihood of explosion if the pressure rises too high
    C) It enables dressings, bedding etc., to be dried before removal.

12. Why is a small-scale automatic autoclave preferable to a manually controlled model?
    A) It is normally much cheaper to run
    B) It operates at a higher temperature and is therefore quicker than, say, a pressure cooker
    C) The human element is eliminated so that the likelihood of error and possible non-sterility is much reduced

13. What particular precaution must be taken in loading a small autoclave not fitted with a vacuum pump?
    A) Enough articles should be included substantially to fill the chamber
    B) Hollow articles should be stacked in it in such a manner that steam can readily enter and displace the air contained in them
    C) Under no account should the water cover any article being sterilised

14. Of all the methods discussed, which of the following is the best available to the small operator?
    A) Dry heat
    B) Moist heat
    C) Propylene oxide

CHAPTER 6

1. Would you regard a pleasant pine-perfumed product, advertised for domestic use, as a possible disinfectant?
   A) Yes
   B) No

2. Very many substances destroy bacteria effectively. Which of the following would be the most important reason why most of them cannot be used for this purpose?
   A) They are often not soluble in water
   B) Many are gases at room temperature
   C) Most are too corrosive or irritant to be acceptable

3. Why must great care be exercised in handling most disinfectants?
   A) They are often very expensive and great care should therefore be taken to avoid waste
   B) Many are explosive and therefore must be kept at low temperature
   C) They are often irritant or allergenic on the skin, and especially in delicate structures such as the eye

4. What is the only criterion which allows the use of disinfection rather than heat sterilisation for a given article?
   A) Price or non-availability of a heat-steriliser
   B) Inconvenience of having to heat up and use a heat-device
   C) Essential equipment is made of materials which would be seriously damaged at heat-sterilising temperatures

5. Why is it important to avoid further dilution of disinfectant/antiseptic solutions when made up for use?
   A) Hard water may cause precipitation of the active substance
   B) The solution may be diluted below its level of effectiveness
   C) The solution may be diluted below its level of effectiveness to the extent that it may itself become infected by some resistant organisms, thus becoming a source of infection

107

6. What is the usual effect of using a disinfectant at a higher temperature than normal?
   A) It is less effective than at room temperature
   B) No difference
   C) It is more effective at higher temperature

7. A solution at pH 5.0 is
   A) acid
   B) alkaline
   C) neutral.

8. What is the effect, in most cases, of having substantial amounts of organic material in a disinfectant?
   A) The effectiveness of the disinfectant is increased
   B) The effectiveness of the disinfectant is decreased
   C) No effect except with phenolic disinfectants

9. What strength of alcohol is most frequently used as a disinfectant/antiseptic?
   A) 100 per cent (absolute alcohol)
   B) 70 per cent
   C) 50 per cent

10. Which TWO of the following alcohols are normally used as antiseptics/disinfectants?
    A) Ethyl alcohol
    B) Methyl alcohol
    C) Isopropyl alcohol
    D) Normal propyl alcohol

11. What are the effects of alcohols on viruses?
    A) They are virucidal
    B) The effect is very limited but varies with the type of virus
    C) No pathogenic viruses are destroyed by alcohol of any strength

12. Which TWO of the following aldehydes are commonly used as disinfectants?
    A) Benzaldehyde
    B) Formaldehyde
    C) Acetaldehyde
    D) Glyeraldehyde
    E) Glutaraldehyde

13. At what strength and pH is glutaraldehyde traditionally used as a disinfectant?
    A) 0.2 per cent, pH 4.0
    B) 2.0 per cent at pH 4.0
    C) 2.0 per cent at about pH 8.0

14. What is the life of traditional activated glutaraldehyde after activation?
    A) 28 days
    B) 14 weeks
    C) 14 or 28 days, depending on type

15. At room temperature, 2 per cent activated glutaraldehyde kills bacterial spores in less than
    A) 3 minutes
    B) 3 hours
    C) 3 days

16. Which of the following is true of 2 per cent activated glutaraldehyde?
    A) It is severely irritant to skin and eyes
    B) It is slightly irritant to skin and severely irritant to eyes
    C) Skin irritation is minimal and it is often used as a mild antiseptic

17. Group the following into three pairs.
    A) Chlorhexidine is known as
    B) Savlon
    C) Dettol
    D) Hibitane
    E) Cetrimide/chlorhexidine mixture is marketed as
    F) Chlorxylenol is the active ingredient of

18. Chlorhexidine is especially suitable for skin disinfection because
    A) it is a valuable detergent as well as a bactericide
    B) treated skin is stained so that the treated area is clearly defined
    C) it tends to bind to skin hence giving a prolonged effect, especially after repeated application.

19. Alcoholic solutions of Hibitane are preferable to aqueous because
    A) tubercle bacillus is not killed by Hibitane but is killed by alcohol
    B) Hibitane is almost insoluble in water hence an effective aqueous solution cannot be prepared
    C) the aqueous solution is more irritant than the alcoholic one.

20. Chlorhexidine is incompatible with
    A) cetrimide
    B) household soap
    C) alcohol.

21. Ten per cent solutions of Domestos to be used for disinfecting worktops etc., should be freshly prepared
    A) hourly
    B) daily
    C) weekly.

22. Apart from their bacteriostatic activity, QACs are valuable as
    A) cationic detergents
    B) anionic detergents
    C) non-ionic detergents.

23. Hexachlorophane is especially valuable as a surgical scrub because
    A) most viruses are susceptible to it
    B) it is most effective against Gram-negative organisms
    C) it is very effective against *Staph. aureus*.

ANSWERS TO SELF-EXAMINATION QUESTIONS

CHAPTER 1

1. C	4. C, D	7. C	10. C	13. AD, BC
2. B	5. B	8. A	11. B	14. A, D, F
3. B	6. B	9. A	12. AC, BD	

CHAPTER 2

1. C	5. C	9. A	13. B	17. C
2. B	6. B	10. A	14. B	18. C
3. B	7. C	11. C	15. A	19. B
4. C	8. A	12. B	16. B	

CHAPTER 3

1. C	5. C	9. B	13. A	17. B
2. C	6. A, E, F	10. A, E	14. B	18. B
3. C	7. C, D	11. B	15. B	19. C
4. C	8. E	12. B	16. A	

CHAPTER 4

1. C	2. B	3. A	4. A	5. B

CHAPTER 5

1. B	4. A, D	7. C	10. B, D	13. B
2. C	5. B	8. C	11. C	14. B
3. C	6. A	9. A	12. C	

CHAPTER 6

1. B	6. C	11. B	16. B	21. B
2. C	7. A	12. B, E	17. AD, EB, FC	22. A
3. C	8. B	13. C	18. C	23. C
4. C	9. B	14. C	19. A	
5. C	10. A, C	15. B	20. B	

CHAPTER 9

Model by-laws

The following are the model by-laws relating to ear-piercing and electrolysis, made in pursuance of section 15.7 of the Local Government (Miscellaneous Provisions) Act 1982 (Crown Copyright). They are reproduced here as a convenient reference and as a useful guide to the standards of hygiene likely to be acceptable in countries other than the UK.

In the UK local authorities are not obliged to introduce by-laws in this form but most do so and copies of the by-laws are available from local authorities or HMSO suppliers.

It will be noted that the law places responsibilities both on the proprietor and the operator.

1. Interpretation

    a) In these by-laws, unless the context otherwise requires –

    'The Act' means the Local Government (Miscellaneous Provisions) Act, 1982;
    'Client' means any person undergoing treatment;
    'Operator' means any person giving treatment;
    'Premises' means any premises registered under Part VIII of the Act;
    'Proprietor' means any person registered under Part VIII of the Act;
    'Treatment' means any operation in effecting ear-piercing or electrolysis;
    'The treatment area' means any part of the premises where treatment is given to clients.

    b) The Interpretation Act 1978 shall apply for the interpretation of these by-laws as it applies for the interpretation of an Act of Parliament.

2. For the purpose of securing the cleanliness of premises and fittings therein a proprietor shall ensure that:

   a) All internal doors, walls, windows, partitions, floors and floor coverings, and ceilings in any part of the premises used by clients and operators are kept clean and in such good repair as to enable them to be cleaned effectively.

   b) All waste material and other litter, arising from treatment, is placed in suitable covered receptacles, which are washable and leakproof, or use a leakproof liner bag. The receptacles shall be emptied, or the bags changed, at least once every working day, or more frequently as necessary, and the material disposed of safely. Where liners are not used, the receptacles shall then be cleaned.

   c) All needles used in treatment are placed after use in separate covered and leakproof reusable boxes, or disposable needle-boxes designed for the purpose. When reusable boxes are used they shall be emptied at least once every working day or more frequently as necessary, and the contents disposed of safely or sterilised for reuse as appropriate. The box shall then be sterilised. Where needle-boxes are used they shall be disposed of safely at suitable intervals.

   d) All furniture and fittings in the treatment area are kept clean and in such good repair as to enable them to be cleaned effectively.

   e) All tables, couches and seats used by clients in the treatment area and any surface on which the items specified in 3b) below are placed immediately prior to treatment have a smooth impervious surface which is wiped down regularly with a suitable disinfectant.

   f) Where tables or couches are used, they shall be covered by a disposable paper sheet which shall be changed for each client.

   g) A notice or notices reading 'No Smoking' are prominently displayed in the treatment area.

3. For the purpose of securing the cleansing and, so far as is appropriate, the sterilisation of instruments, materials and equipment used in connection with the treatment

   a) An operator shall ensure that, before use in connection with treatment, any gown, wrap or other protective clothing, paper or other covering, towel, cloth or other such articles used in the treatment
      i) is clean and in good repair, and, so far as is appropriate, is sterile;
      ii) has not previously been used in connection with any other client unless it consists of a material which can be and has been adequately cleaned and, so far as is appropriate, sterilised.

   b) An operator shall ensure that any needle, metal instrument or other item of equipment used in treatment or for handling instruments and needles used in treatment is in a sterile condition and kept sterile until used.

   c) A proprietor shall provide
      i) adequate facilities and equipment for the purposes of sterilisation (unless pre-sterilised items are used) and of cleansing, as required in pursuance of these by-laws;
      ii) sufficient and safe gas points and/or electrical socket outlets to enable compliance with these by-laws;
      iii) an adequate supply of clean hot and cold water readily available at all times on the premises;
      iv) adequate storage of all items mentioned in by-law 3a) and b) above, so that these items shall be properly stored in a clean and suitable place so as to avoid as far as possible the risk of contamination.

4. For the purpose of securing the cleanliness of operators

   a) An operator, whilst giving treatment shall ensure that
      i) his hands are clean;
      ii) he is wearing clean clothing;
      iii) he keeps any open boil, sore, cut or open wound on an exposed part of his body effectively covered by an impermeable dressing;
      iv) he does not smoke or consume food or drink;

b) A proprietor shall provide
   i) suitable and sufficient washing facilities for the use of operators, such facilities to have hot and cold water, sanitising soap or detergent, and a nail brush;
   ii) suitable and sufficient sanitary accommodation for operators.

CHAPTER 10

Recommended supplementary reading

There are few books on sterilisation and hygiene written specifically for workers in the health-care or beauty fields. With the exception of 'A Guide to Hygienic Skin Piercing', the books mentioned below are written for other professions, primarily medicine and nursing. In the list that follows, an attempt is made to classify the books by subject but this is not always possible since most cover a broad range of related subjects.

MICROBIOLOGY

These books usually include additional information about disease and immune systems:

C. J. A. Thomas, *Medical Microbiology* 6th edition, (Baillière Tindall, 1988).

Although written for medical students this is an eminently readable book embracing all the ground mentioned above.

L. McKane and J. Kandel, *Microbiology – Essentials and Applications*, (McGraw-Hill, 1986).

Brock, Smith and Madigan, *Biology of Micro-organisms* 5th edition, (Prentice-Hall, 1988).

The latter two books are advanced and comprehensive.

VIROLOGY

Dimmock and Primrose, *Introduction to Modern Virology* 3rd edition, (Blackwell Scientific Publications, 1987).

M. C. Timbury, *Notes on Medical Virology*, (Churchill Livingstone, 1986).

The latter covers viruses and virus diseases including AIDS and hepatitis.

MEDICAL ENTOMOLOGY

M. W. Service, *Lecture Notes on Medical Entomology*, (Blackwell Scientific Publications, 1986).

J. H. Grundy, *Arthropods of Medical Importance*, (Noble Books Ltd, 1981).

AIDS

D. Miller, *Living with AIDS and HIV*, (The MacMillan Press Ltd, 1988).

A simply written general purpose book.

British Medical Bulletin Vol. 44, No. 1, January 1988, 'AIDS and HIV Infection – the wider perspective', edited by A. J. Pinching, R. A. Weiss, and D. Miller, (Churchill Livingstone for the British Council).

A useful book covering the wider aspects of AIDS and HIV infection.

ABC of AIDS, edited by M. W. Adler, (British Medical Journal, 1987).

A book containing abstracts of articles published in the *British Medical Journal*.

DISINFECTION AND STERILISATION

R. B. Calmes Jnr. and T. Lillach, *Disinfection and Sterilization in Dental Practice*, (McGraw-Hill, 1978).

Dental equipment is on much the same scale as that used in beauty therapy and by health care workers and much of the information given is relevant to these professionals whilst being fairly simply written.

Isobel M. Maurer, *Hospital Hygiene*, (Edward Arnold, 1985).

This is intended for hospital personnel but has a practical, common sense approach to the subject which readers may find helpful.

Disinfection, Sterilization and Preservation 3rd edition, edited by S. S. Block, (Lea and Febiger, Philadelphia, PA, 1983).

This is a very comprehensive and advanced book for consultation by the serious student.

Martindale, *The Extra Pharmacopoeia*, 28th edition, (Pharmaceutical Press, 1982).

This is a reference book covering drugs in general use including sections on all the substances in common use for disinfection and antiseptics.

OTHER BOOKS AND PAMPHLETS

N. D. Noah, *A Guide to Hygienic Skin Piercing*, (PHLS Communicable Disease Surveillance Centre, 1983).

This book is out of print at the time of writing and a revised edition is awaited. It summarises recommended procedures for those engaged in tattooing, ear-piercing, acupuncture and electrolysis.

Guidelines for Hygienic Hairdressing is available from the PHLS Communicable Disease Surveillance Centre, 61 Colindale Avenue, London, NW9 5EQ.

A further guidelines series is issued by the Department of Health and Social Security and copies can be ordered in the UK by telephoning 0800 555 777 (Central Office of Information, Hercules Road, London SE1 7DU). The following titles are available:

Guidelines for electrolysists
Guidelines for acupuncturists
Guidelines for unregistered chiropodists
Guidelines for ear piercers
Guidelines for hairdressers and barbers
Guidelines for tattooists

These relate specifically to risk of AIDS infection in relation to the professions listed.

Appendices

APPENDIX 1 – MICROSCOPES

There are two main types of microscope, the optical or light microscope and the electron microscope.

The optical microscope is the classical one and is a lens system illuminated by light. Its magnification is limited by the wavelength of light – it cannot produce a detailed image of objects less than about half the wavelength of light (0.25 μm). Thus although the smallest bacteria may be seen, their finer detail cannot be distinguished. Viruses cannot be seen. There are variants in technique for various purposes – ultraviolet and phase-contrast microscopy and dark-ground techniques.

The electron microscope replaces light by a beam of electrons which behave as rays of very short wavelength. The lenses are replaced by magnetic fields. The object is examined in a vacuum and is viewed on a television-type screen. The scanning electron microscope produces even better three-dimensional images.

APPENDIX 2 – ALKALINITY AND ACIDITY

The term pH is used as a convenient way of indicating relative acidity or alkalinity. pH 7 is neutral and pH levels lower than this are acid – the lower the number, the greater the acidity. A pH of more than seven indicates alkalinity – the more alkaline a solution, the higher the number – up to a limit of pH 14.

Often the pH is easily upset and it may be important to keep it within certain limits. To do this a chemical known as a **buffer** is added to the solution. Buffering at a given pH may increase the stability of a product or may be necessary to achieve maximum effectiveness.

APPENDIX 3 – NOT AN IDEAL CLINIC OR SALON!
(Page 84)

The following are the more obvious hazards of hygiene in this clinic or salon. You may find some more!

Operator
a) She has long, untidy hair which could well sweep across the client's face, or the area being treated, carrying infection.
b) Her overall has long sleeves which could easily become infected and transfer infection to the client.
c) She has loose jewellery about her wrists and fingers which could become infected, as well as unnecessary ornamentation on her overall.
d) With her overall partly unbuttoned, she presents a general air of carelessness and untidiness.

Fittings
a) UV Steriliser – there is no such thing as an ultraviolet steriliser. At best there is a limited disinfectant effect from UV radiation and its use is limited to the reduction of the bacterial content of air in special circumstances.
b) Large bottles should not be kept on high level shelves or the top of a treatment trolley, especially if unstoppered, where they may be knocked over on to the client.
c) Sufficient electric wall-sockets should be fitted. The one shown is grossly overloaded and trailing wires represent a hazard in several respects, including harbouring dust and impeding proper cleaning.
d) There is no wash-hand basin and hand-drier for the use of the operator.
e) There does not appear to be a receptacle for used swabs, etc. Most of them seem to have been dropped on to the floor!

Treatment trolley
a) This is grossly cluttered with unnecessary articles. There are discarded cotton wool swabs in several places and none of the needle-containers have lids. It is difficult to distinguish between the container of sterile needles and that for used needles. There appears to be no paper tissue on which to place the in-use needle-holder and forceps. The large unstoppered bottle on the top shelf has been mentioned above.

b) There is a cup and saucer on the bottom shelf. Food and drink must *never* be allowed in the treatment area. It can readily become infected from the operator's hands and infection transferred to her mouth.
c) There is a well-filled ash-tray and burning cigarette on the top shelf. Smoking should *never* be permitted in the treatment areas since it carries the same risk of causing cross-infection as does food.

Food, drink and smoking are prohibited in treatment areas by the model by-laws in the UK.

General
There is a general air of untidiness about the room which suggests lack of care by the operator. Such conditions must indicate a poor attitude towards hygiene and the chances of such an outlook producing cross-infection risks are very high.

The cat might be useful for catching the mice, but animals must never be admitted to the treatment room, they can carry dirt and infection.

Although some may feel it unnecessary, if the client's shoes rest on the actual treatment chair, it would seem preferable to remove them and use a renewable paper sheet on the chair.

Perhaps the client's somewhat apprehensive look is justified!

Index

Acid-fast bacteria   6
Acridines   81
Aerobes   4
Aflatoxin   25
AIDS (Acquired Immune Deficiency Syndrome)   40-2
Alcohols,   71-4, 94, 95
Aldehydes   74-7
Alkalinity and acidity   119
Anaerobes   4, 7
Antibiotic   46
Antibodies   8-9, 35-6
Antigens   8-9, 36
Antiseptics   44, 67-82, 95
Arbovirus   21
Arthropods   27-8
Attenuated bacteria and viruses   34
Ascaris lumbricoides   26
Aseptic methods   39, 46
Aspergillus   25
Autoclaves, steam   48, 57, 58-65
Autotrophs   4
AZT (zidovudine)   42

Bacilli
   genus   3
   Gram-negative   13
   Gram-positive   11
   rod-form of bacteria   5
   B. subtilis, bacteriological monitoring   49
Bacteria   1-15
   staining processes   6
Bactericide   45
Bacteriophages   16
Bacteriostat   45
Betadine   80
Bilirubin   37
Binary fission   1
Binomial classification   4
Biocide   45
Biostat   45
Blood plasma   35
Bowie-Dick test   48
British Standard Glossary of Terms relating to Disinfectants (BS 5283 of 1976)   43

Browne's tubes   48
Browne's TST strips   48
Buffers, pH   69-70, 119

Candida albicans   24
Capsid   17
Capsule, bacterial   2
Carriers, symptomless   31-2
Cetavlon   81
Cetrimide   81
Cell wall, bacterial   1, 2
Cell-mediated defences   18, 35-6
Certificates of registration, and competence   89
Chemosteriliser, glutaraldehyde as   76
Chlamydiae   9
Chloramines   79
Chlorhexidine   77-8
Chlorine   79, 94
Chlorxylenol   80
Cidex   75
Cleaning, before sterilisation   49-50
Clostridia   3, 12
   contamination by spores of   73, 78
Cobalt-60, source of gamma-irradiation   51
Cocci   5, 11
Commensals   9, 31, 35
Complement   35
Cold sterilising solutions   47
Colonies (of bacteria)   6
Couches, treatment, paper coverings for   91, 113
Coxiellae   9
Cross-infection   29, 36, 42
   and skin-piercing   33-4
Crystal violet   81
Culture media   6-8

Dark field technique (microscopy)   15
Daughter cells, bacterial   3
Defences, body's, against infection   34-6
Deoxyribonucleic acid (DNA)   2
Dermatophytes   24
Detergents, anionic, cationic and non-ionic   81
Dettol   80
Dideoxycytidine   42

Diguanides 77-8
Diphyllobothrium latum 27
Disinfectants 44, 67-82
Disinfection, as alternative to sterilisation 68
Dispray 2 78, 94
Domestos 79
Downward displacement (of cold air in autoclaves) 59

Endotoxins 8
Enterobius vermicularis 26
Envelope, viral 17
Enzymes 2
Epidermophyton 24
Equipment, choice of 86-8, 90, 91
 disinfection and sterilisation of 93-4
Ethyl alcohol 71, 72, 73
Ethylene oxide 52
Escherichia coli (E. coli) 31
Exotoxins 8

Favus 24
Fimbria 2
Flagellum 2
Flaming, as a sterilising method 55
Floor surfaces for treatment areas 91, 113
Formaldehyde 52, 75
Formalin 75
Fungi 24-5
Fungicide 45
Fungistat 45

Gamma irradiation, colour change markers 49
 sterilising method 51
Gases, as sterilising agents 52
Genes 2
Gentian violet 81
Genus 4
Glass bead sterilisers 55-6
Glutaraldehyde 75-7
 and equipment disinfection 93-4
 sporicidal activity 68, 75
 virucidal activity 69
Gram's stain 6

Halogens 79-80
 virucidal activity 69
HAV (hepatitis A virus) 23, 37-8
HBsAg 38
HBV (hepatitis B virus) 23, 37, 38-9
Heating-up time, in heat sterilisation 53
Heat penetration time, in heat sterilisation 53
Heat, dry, as a sterilising method 54-6

Heat, moist, as a sterilising agent 57-65
 temperature ranges required 57, 58
 temperature/time exposures (MRC recommendations) 58
Helminths *see* Worms
Hepatitis 37-40
Hepatitis A 37-8
Hepatitis B 38-9
 routes of infection 33-4
Hepatitis, non-A, non-B 37, 39
Heterotrophs 4
Hexachlorophane 80
Hibiscrub 78
Hibisol 78
Hibitane *see* chlorhexidine
High energy electrons, sterilising method 50
HIV (Human Immunodeficiency Virus) 23, 40-2
Holding time, in heat sterilisation 53
8-hydroxyquinoline 81
Hygienic procedures, design of 83-96
Hypochlorites, of calcium and sodium 79

Icosahedral 22
Immunity, acquired 35-6
Immunoglobulins (Ig) 35
Immunosuppression 41
Incineration, as a sterilising method 55
Industrial methylated spirit (IMS) 71-2
Infection 29-42
 opportunistic, and AIDS 41
Influenza 23, 31
Inoculation, prophylactic 34
Interferon 20, 35
Invasiveness 8
Iodine 79, 80
Iodophores 80
Isopropyl alcohol 71

Jaundice 37

Kaposi's sarcoma 41

Latent heat of vaporisation 57
Legal requirements, in skin piercing work 88-9
 in disinfection and sterilising of equipment 93
 Model by-laws 112-15
Lice, body and head 28
Linnaean classification 4
Local Government (Miscellaneous Provisions) Act, 1982 88-9
 Model by-laws pursuant to section 15.7 of 112-15
Lymphocytes 35, 36, 41

123

Macrophages 35
Malachite green 81
Malassezia furfur 24
Masks, surgical, use of 33
Mean generation time 3
Mercury compounds 81
Methyl alcohol 71, 74
Methylated spirit 71-2
Micrometre 5
Microscopes, optical and electron 119
Microsporum 24
Milton 79
Mycelium 24
Mycoplasmas 9
  M. pneumoniae 9
Mycobacterium tuberculosis 12, 75, 78, 79, 80, 81

Needles, skin piercing 86, 87-8, 113
  in transmission of disease 36
  self-testing on operators 94
Needle-stick injuries, avoidance of 88, 95
Nits 28
Nanometre 17

Operators, personal cleanliness and protection 95
  duties imposed upon, in model by-laws 114
Opportunistic infections in AIDS 41
Ovens, hot air, for sterilising 54

Parenteral route, of infection 33
Pathogenic 4
Pediculus species 28
pH 119
Phagocytes and phagocytosis 35
Phenols 80
Pili 2
Pneumocystis carinii 25, 41
Polyhedron 17
Polymers and polymerisation 75
Polymorphs (polymorphonuclear leucocytes) 35
Povidone iodine 80
Pressure cookers, use as autoclaves 62
β-propiolactone 81
Proprietors of skin-piercing establishments
  duties imposed upon by model by-laws 114, 115
Propylene oxide, sterilising agent 52
Protista 25
Protoplast 1

Pseudomonas species 14
  resistance to QAC/diguanide combinations 81
Pthirus pubis 28

Quaternary ammonium compounds (Quats, QACs) 81
QAC/diguanide combinations 81

Radiation (sterilising method) 50-1
Reticulo-endothelial system 35
Reverse transcriptase 23, 42
Ribonucleic acid (RNA) 16
Rickettsiae 9
Ringworm, hair and skin 24-5
Risks associated with treatments, assessment of 85

Safety time, in heat sterilisation 53
Salmonella 7, 13, 31-2
Saprophytes 25
Sarcoptes scabiei 28
Savlon 81
Scabies 28
Seroconversion 36
Seropositive 36
'Sharps', dangers in cleaning 50
  disposal of 91-3, 113
Skin-piercing procedures in transmission of diseases 36
Smoking, forbidden in treatment areas 113
Species 4
Spirochaetes 15
Spores, bacterial 3
  fungal 24
Sporicide 45
Staphylococci 10, 11, 33
  Staph. aureus 10, 11, 80
Steam 57-9, 63
Sterilisation 47-66
Sterilising time, in heat sterilisation 53
Sterilisers, glass bead 55
  hot air 54
  instrument 57
Streptococci 11, 33
Surface active agents 81
Surgical spirit 71-2

Taenia saginata 26-7
  T. solium 27
Thermal death time (TDT) 53
Tinea pedis, capitis 24
  cruris 25
Tissue-cultures 20-1

Toxicity   8
Toxins   8
Toxoids   9
Treponema pallidum   15
Trichomonas vaginalis   25
Trichophyton   24
TST strips   48
   in small autoclaves and pressure cookers   62, 64, 65, 66

Ultrasonic cleaning   50
Ultraviolet light, in control of micro-organisms   51
UV cabinets   51, 84, 120

Vegetative form, of bacteria   3
Virucide   45

Virulence (of bacteria)   8
Viruses   16-23
   antigenicity   20
   DNA viruses   22
   mutation   20
   reproduction and invasiveness   18
   RNA viruses   22-3
   RNA-DNA viruses   23

Wall coverings for treatment areas   91, 113
Washing facilities for operators   90-1
Waste, disposal of   91-3, 113
Working environment, choice of   90-1
Worms   26-7

Zidovudine (AZT)   42
Ziehl-Neelsen stain   6